A Masonic Evolution
The New World of Freemasonry

by Michael R. Poll

A Cornerstone Book

A Masonic Evolution
The New World of Freemasonry
by Michael R. Poll

A Cornerstone Book
Published by Cornerstone Book Publishers
Copyright © 2018 - 2022 by Michael R. Poll

Cornerstone Book Publishers
Hot Springs Village, AR

First Cornerstone Edition - 2018
Second Cornerstone Edition 2021
Third Cornerstone Edition 2022

www.cornerstonepublishers.com

ISBN: 978-1-887560-64-1

Table of Contents

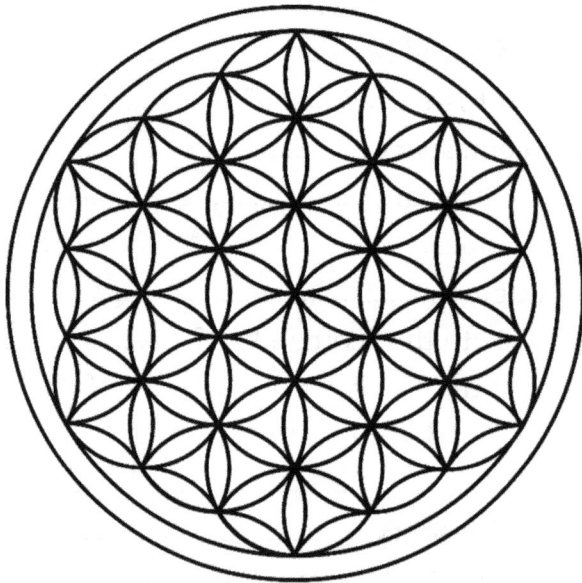

Introduction

Every morning we get up and begin our day. We fill it with whatever we do and then night falls. We have no control over the beginning and ending of each day. But we do have a choice in how we spend our time. We can do good things, bad things, or nothing at all. We can try to advance ourselves and society, or not. It's our choice. No matter what we do, or don't do, the time will pass. One day we will be gone. We will no longer be able to help ourselves or others. What a shame it will be if our life turns out to be a waste.

Freemasonry is going through a time of evolution. That's clear. But where is it going? It may be changing into something new, going back to what it was, or just stirring the pot. I don't know. But I do know that it needs us all. It needs Freemasons who are willing to step up and learn, teach, and evolve with Freemasonry. We can't just wear a ring and show up to sit on the sidelines of lodge meetings. Well, we can do that, but it will be a Masonic waste. It is a time for positive action. It is a time for Masons to *be* Masons and do what is necessary for our Craft.

In this book, I have tried to present my beliefs on what we should be doing and learning. Who we are today and some of our past is explored. I'm trying to the best of my ability to do my part in the Great Work. If this book is of some little help to anyone reading it, then I am truly rewarded. Join me in the Masonic evolution.

May you grow in Light.

Michael R. Poll
Spring, 2018

A Masonic Evolution
The New World of Freemasonry

The Ancient Mystery Schools

We often hear that Freemasonry is tied to the Ancient Mystery Schools through initiation. This presents us with several basic and important questions. What were the Ancient Mystery Schools and what is initiation?

Early man lived off the land and hunted for the food that he needed. Groups of humans would gather for both protection and social interaction. From all that we can gather from available information, there was always a realization that there was something more and greater, whose hand guided all actions and creations. There was also the desire to reach out and touch the unknown.

In some of the earliest records and archaeological evidence we can find traces of humans practicing various ceremonies and initiations. These initiations could be part of a child growing into adult hood, ceremonies following death, or individuals simply seeking something greater out of life. In all cases, there was a desire to be something more. Why such a desire existed, we don't know. Why there has always been a deep feeling in humans that there *was* something more, we don't know.

We can find many examples of initiation in numerous ancient societies and groups. One of the common threads through all these examples is that there are, most often, three similar conditions that are required for an initiation to be considered valid. These three conditions are a desire to initiate, a desire *to be* initiated, and the proper setting.

If we look at a Masonic lodge and examine how we initiate candidates, we can find the same three conditions of initiation in practice in our lodges. When a candidate petitions to join Masonry that is the desire *to be initiated*. He has taken an active step of his own free will. When a lodge ballots on and accepts a petition that is *the desire to initiate*. The proper setting of a lodge is when an initiation takes place with the membership being respectful of the initiation and void of humor or distracting side discussions.

There is a thought that when one receives a proper initiation, a door is opened for them. But a door to what? The suggestion is that the door leads to another room — a symbolic room of enlightenment, spiritual growth, and wisdom. But initiation itself does not give us these things; it only makes them available.

Rosicrucian philosophy speaks of one identified as the Dweller on the Threshold. This individual stands in an open doorway, but he does not enter the next room. He stands outside of the room filled with wonderful things. He does not take advantage of any of it by simply taking the next step of walking into the room.

Initiation is not the end goal for the true Seeker of Light. Initiation only opens the door for us, but it is required for us to walk in and use the initiation as a means of advancing ourselves and gaining enlightenment. The responsibility of action is ours.

Wisdom through initiation was often a lifelong process for the initiates in many of the ancient, enlightened cultures. A great center of wisdom was Alexandria, Egypt. Every imaginable area of enlightened study was available to students in Alexandria. Alexandria was located on the main trade routes and the area brought in many seeking greater knowledge of the esoteric arts. The hidden and reserved teachings from around the world were gathered, studied, and preserved in Alexandria.

But there was another important aspect of Alexandria. It was the large complex of libraries. The libraries of Alexandria are the most famous in antiquity and most likely the largest ever assembled in ancient times. The libraries are said to have contained over a million documents containing the wisdom of the ancient worlds. When these libraries were destroyed, humanity was deprived of more knowledge than we can possibly ever realize.

The destruction of these libraries also sealed off from us the source of the wisdom contained in these libraries. It is very possible that the source of the wisdom contained in these libraries were the libraries themselves. Enlightened initiates may have used these libraries not only as a source of knowledge, but as research centers where theories could be studied and developed. But all that remains today are rumors, stories, and fables about the libraries and through them, with them, and because of them, the ancient mystery schools.

It is puzzling that it was not until the early 1800s that any serious attempt was made at studying the Egyptian hieroglyphics. This presents us with the obvious question that if so little was known of ancient Egyptian language at the foundation and early days of speculative Freemasonry, then why does so much of our ritual so closely resemble ancient Egyptian ritual? Where did the early speculative Freemasons derive this knowledge? Suggestions that it could be coincidence border on the irrational. Even the mention of the Ancient Mystery Schools in our Masonic teachings suggests some tie to the schools. And what is the tie? Initiation.

Given the vast amount of what we do not know of our early history, I do not believe that it is that great a leap to suggest that ancient teachings, including those of initiation, traveled down through ancient times, through the Operative Masons and developed into what we know as Speculative Freemasonry.

The ancient mystery schools can be looked at as a collection of formal or informal bodies of esoteric instruction. We can assume that to gain admission to one of these *schools* a candidate would need to pass a rigorous screening and examination into their character. Following an examination into their worthiness, they would take part in an initiation or some form of a Rite of Passage.

We can look at so many aspects of our Masonic initiation as well as our Masonic philosophy and teachings to realize that much of it is archaic. Our settings, furniture, symbols, words, and practices do seem to come from a different place and time. It is not difficult to see the similarities between our Hiramic legend and the legend of

Osiris. It is not difficult to see many ancient teachings, traditions and symbols borrowed by Freemasonry from long-lost civilizations. But who were these civilizations?

Based on new discoveries and research, it seems that our understanding of ancient Egypt would seem to need complete reexamination and rethought.

Its level of scientific expertise and cultural development appear to be much greater than what is accepted by classical academia. Look at the massive and perplexing Sphinx. It was built during a time when there was not supposed to be any civilization in the area at all. What technology was there in place at the time of the building of the Sphinx? We have no idea.

Look at what we know of very early Egyptian language, religion, and philosophy. At the beginning of the old Kingdom and the first pharaohs, we see there an *intact hieroglyphic* system, which was their complete writing system. We also see a *complex* science, religion, and philosophy. Their whole system seems to have been there at the very beginning of the old Kingdom. How is that possible? How is it possible to begin something as complex as the ancient Egyptian society with everything in place at the very beginning?

Rare and very early documents suggest much older advanced civilizations existed long prior to the time of the old Kingdom. Maybe these older civilizations contributed to what would become their language and society. These very ancient and advanced civilizations may have been responsible for the building of many of the wonderful structures attributed to ancient Egypt. Clearly, there is so very much that we simply do not know.

But let's now look at the often misunderstood and equally mysterious Rosicrucians. The famous Brotherhood of the Rosy Cross. For the uninitiated, it is said that to try and understand the Rosicrucians is to try and grab handfuls of smoke. While it is sometimes difficult to sort the history from the lore, there are certain aspects of the Rosicrucians that we can look at and study — from a certain perspective.

Rosicrucianism has long been associated with both Freemasonry and the Ancient Mystery Schools. It has been suggested that the Rosicrucians and the Freemasons are something of first cousins. The fact is that trying to understand the early history of the Rosicrucians is as difficult as trying to understand the early history of Freemasonry.

While the history of both orders is obscured and difficult to impossible to completely understand, there is a thread that runs through the philosophy of both Orders that is kindred and somewhat traceable. An old Rosicrucian thought is that either one has always been a Rosicrucian, or they never will be one. While this statement makes no sense from an organizational standpoint, if we look at it from a philosophical view, then it takes on new meaning.

The suggestion would seem to be that it is the Rosicrucian *philosophy*, not the organization, which is at the heart of being a Rosicrucian. One is a Rosicrucian if they embrace its philosophy. Like Freemasonry, the Rosicrucian philosophy seems to have a life of its own separate and apart from the organization.

Also, like Freemasonry, the Rosicrucian Order has a distinct Egyptian flavor to it. Much of its philosophy, rituals, symbols, teachings, and even art is Egyptian in nature. Again, like Freemasonry, the Rosicrucians Order draws an association between itself and a particular medieval order, the Knights Templer. The Rose Croix, the Rosy Cross, the Order Rosae Crucis — they all have the same theme, design and suggestion. They are the Order of the Red Cross.

But there is no clear answer *as to why*.

Faint lines… rarely traceable, do seem connect these secretive Orders, and for those capable of connecting obscured dots, trace what we have today, through esoteric philosophy, to the very early days of man. And what connects them all, is initiation.

In very ancient Egypt, the all-seeing eye was known as the Eye of Horus or the Eye of Ra. Through various myths this was a symbol of healing, protection, and wisdom. The left eye of Horus was said to be the moon and the right eye the sun. Some have suggested that the right and left "all-seeing eyes" reflect the two known descendants of the Ancient Mystery Schools: the Rosicrucians and the Freemasons.

If the suggestion is that the Ancient Mystery Schools, the great temple at Karnack, transformed from a place of esoteric instruction into an active Order with the goal of preserving sacred wisdom and transmitting to it to future generations, then it is not difficult to see a very unscientific and unproven chain of transmission. We can see early Jewish and Christian mystery traditions, including (but hardly limited to) the Nazarenes, the Essenes, the Jacobites, the

Templars, the Operative Masons, the Rosicrucians, and Speculative Freemasonry, all passing on a secret tradition, a wisdom, a philosophy to future generations of initiates.

It would be naïve to suggest that we have many, if any, real answers. We can be likened to a fully grown man with a rich, full history, but one with amnesia. All the details of his life would exist, but they would be unknown to him. But this is only when we examine ancient Egyptian traditions. Ancient Eastern traditions also exist. The Hindus and Buddhists and many others also have rich esoteric traditions.

In India, an ancient Sanskrit text informs us that the Hindu god Shiva has three eyes. One Rosicrucian writer suggests that this third all seeing eye reflects in, Western esoteric tradition, the triad of the Western ancient mystery schools which include the Rosicrucians, the Freemasons, and the Roman Catholic Church. All three have ceremonies of initiation, teach through symbolic lessons, and preserve wisdom to pass on to future generations.

Is any of this provable through scientific examination? Not at all. But prove that you love the Almighty. There are limits as to what can be proven through science, but no limits as to what is acceptable to a belief system. The poet Khalil Gibran once wrote, "Faith is a knowledge within the heart, beyond the reach of proof." We must have science to keep us grounded, but if we are to have true balance then we must also have the creative imagination of a child and the courage to believe, even if what we believe cannot be proven through science.

If Freemasonry is only a club for the social enjoyment of our members and if our ceremonies of initiation are only plays designed to entertain and mimic things that we don't understand, then nothing that we do is of any great importance. We might as well entertain ourselves in better ways. Certainly, there are many more ways that we can entertain ourselves that are more satisfying than listening to minutes or arguing over bills.

But if Freemasonry is more than a club then maybe it is worth a closer look. I believe that we are *much* more than a club. Initiation is that element within us that not only ties us to the Ancient Mystery Schools but makes the past as relevant today as it was in ancient times.

It is clear to me that our Masonic initiation, when properly done, opens that mystic or spiritual door for us and gives us the opportunity to explore much deeper aspects of ourselves. It's up to us if we want to walk through that door leading to deeper corners of ourselves, enlighten ourselves, explore ourselves, and grow to our limits. No one will force us. In fact, many times only a few are aware of exactly what we have in our initiations. They are *themselves* as the Dweller on the Threshold — at best! We must understand that there are times when our leaders and teachers will be woefully ignorant of the treasure that is at our fingertips. It doesn't matter who is at fault for this situation. It simply exists.

There are a few things sadder than seeing the opportunity of initiation wasted because individuals, with no clue as to the true nature of Freemasonry, use our ceremonies as sources of entertainment. The candidate may not be aware that anything has gone wrong, but he will also likely not be aware of that *special something* that many candidates feel when initiation *is* done properly. Placing blame and insulting either the unknowing or the knowing who allowed the levity or distractions is of little benefit. We must see Masonic initiation as a responsibility, an honor, and a gift that we must share.

What we have in Freemasonry is clearly very old. It has been clearly very important to many people for a very long time. This does not mean that we can prove an actual lineage to anything. If we believe the skeptics, there may be nothing of any value in an initiation — no matter if it is done properly or improperly. On the other hand, maybe it is far more important, far older, and far more significant than we have any idea.

I, for one, believe that valid Masonic initiation is one of the keys to a rewarding life. I believe that in all aspects of the lodge, we are to show respect, care, and reverence.

The Voice of One

Recently, I travelled to Pennsylvania to join *The Journal of The Masonic Society's* Art Director John Bridegroom at a meeting of the Pennsylvania Academy of Masonic Knowledge. We were both invited to lecture at this event. It was my first time visiting Pennsylvania and the first time, in many years, that I had flown. I was sitting in a window seat as the plane was taking off. I marveled to myself at the sight of all the people, cars, and buildings becoming so very small. Cars travelling on roads soon looked like tiny quickly moving toys. Looking down at everything from so high up in the air, I began to think of people quite differently. A strange feeling came over me. What is the true significance of the individual? From that height, I could barely see the cars, much less the people driving them. The people were tiny specks on a great expanse of land. How could any single one of them have any true significance? Are we simply individually unimportant parts of a hive mentality, with maybe a super dose of ego?

Most of the flight I pondered on the question of the importance of the individual. I came to realize that my perspective of people had changed due to my seeing them as tiny specks from my airplane window. But I soon came to see my perspective as faulty. Yes, people were reduced to tiny specks, and it did become easy to discount such seemingly insignificant creatures as being capable of having any real impact on such a large world. The problem was equating size with potential or ability. Throughout history such "tiny specks" have had tremendous impact (for good or bad) on the entire world. I did a good bit of thinking on that trip.

In Freemasonry, the rank-and-file Masons sometimes believe themselves to be these "tiny specks." They sometimes feel that they have no voice of any importance. The perception is sometimes that it is only those of high rank or office who have any voice in Freemasonry. In truth, those who choose not to speak will not have a voice. In the great scheme of things, the only voices that are remembered are the ones that clearly bring about change. A leader who is only concerned with getting through his term of office with as little hassle as possible has a temporary voice because of his office, but he will be soon forgotten when his term ends. In time, even his name will not be remembered except, maybe, by the most dedicated historians. The leaders who will be remembered will be those who stand up and do something. Of course, a leader who rises above the crowd because of noteworthy *bad* actions will also be remembered. Adolf Hitler is certainly remembered, but who wants to be memorialized as him? The leaders who are remembered positively are the ones who stood up and did things of service and benefit for all.

The concept that the rank-and-file Mason has no voice is a misleading belief. We all have a voice. Even if we have no office, rank, or authority, we have a voice. Our choice is to use it or not. Of course, the argument can be made that once we do use our voice, and if it is heard and influences the masses, then we are no longer a rank-and-file Mason; we become a leader ourselves. The belief that the voice of one who has no position of authority is unable to be heard is a false belief. When we speak to the hearts of others, and if our words are sound, then we will be heard no matter if we do or do not have rank or position.

Without question, the single, lone voice of wisdom, logic, and reason has always been heard. Throughout history we see the single voice of hope and solutions being not only heard but followed. In Freemasonry, I truly believe that our job is to learn and then to teach. If we have done our job of learning well, then what we teach will be received. We do have a voice, and it is our responsibility to use it.

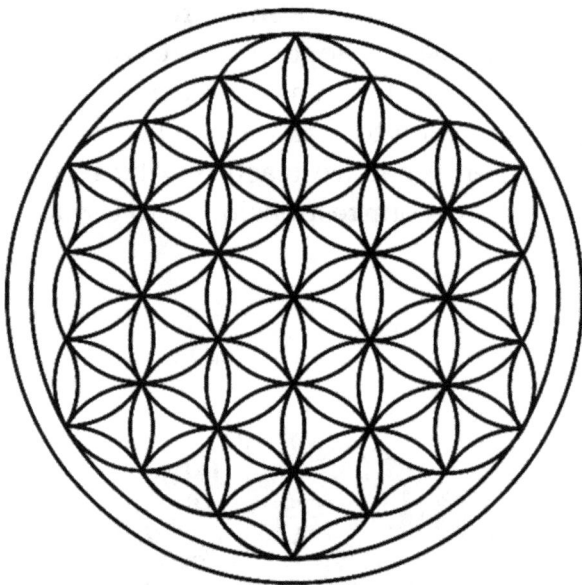

Beginning and Balancing Masonic Education

I've been thinking lately about the practical problem of starting an educational program in a lodge that has been without Masonic education for, maybe, more than a few years. To give you an example, I spoke with a young Mason not too long ago, and he told me of a frustrating experience he had when he asked his lodge if he could conduct an educational program for them. The lodge had gone for many years with only opening the lodge, reading minutes, paying bills, a bit of discussion as to things going on, and then closing. They had no idea what the young Brother meant by "Masonic education," but allowed him to do it mainly because he seemed so eager, and it seemed harmless.

The Brother told me of his great disappointment and frustration when his talk, titled: "The Alchemical References in our Masonic Ritual," was met with blank stares and the entire subject being dismissed as nonsense by nearly everyone present. The Masons in attendance were, clearly, wholly unprepared for such a talk and had no prior experience with the subject. For them, it came out of left field and was outside of all their experiences in Freemasonry.

But let's step back for a minute and try to look at the situation without pointing fingers or trying to take sides. On one hand, you have a young enthusiastic Mason with a desire to both learn and teach the deeper aspects of Freemasonry. On the other, you have a group of Masons whose entire lodge experience has been void of any Masonic education at all, save, maybe, basic ritual. For them, Freemasonry is a business meeting and visiting with a handful of friends several times a month. Nothing more of Freemasonry is known by them.

The expectations of Freemasonry on both sides were completely different. So, what do you do?

Young Masons wanting more out of Freemasonry are frustrated by what seems to be a total lack of substance in the lodge. For the older members, what is being offered by the young members is contrary to everything they know themselves about Freemasonry. Because the older members have rank and authority in the lodge, they sometimes shut down the young Brothers because of feelings that they are trying to modify or improperly introduce what is little more than perceived nonsense into what *they* know of Freemasonry.

Objectively, the lacking is on both sides. Many of the older Masons were simply never taught what they should have been taught at the beginning of their Masonic careers. But these older Masons can't be just disregarded and treated as ignorant Masonic pretenders.

Many of the younger Masons fail to realize that if not for the dedication to Freemasonry by the older Brothers, the lodges would likely have closed long before the young

Brothers would have had a chance to join. Both sides need to stop, step back, and take a breath. Even if a Masonic lodge has had no educational programs in the last twenty-five or more years, it does not mean that education is not important. Nor does it mean that it is impossible to introduce meaningful Masonic education into lodges.

Ego cannot allow senior Masons to prevent Masonic education simply because those who are presenting it are junior to them. By the same turn, young Masons must realize that even though they know and desire some of the deeper aspects of Freemasonry, the senior members are due respect as they have kept the lodge alive – even if it is only on life support.

No responsible educator would attempt to teach trigonometry to a child who cannot count. This is not to say that senior Masons who have never received any serious Masonic education should be treated as children. But we must realize that we cannot run before we can walk.

We must all realize the disadvantage that some of the senior Masons have because *they* were never given what they should have been given by their instructors. Many of the senior Masons were outright short-changed by those before them. We cannot take Masonic education too fast, nor should we start anywhere but with the basics of Masonic education when beginning such a program.

A sound Masonic education program should begin with the basics that are necessary for all Masonic lodges. In fact, most of the problems faced by lodges come from an embarrassing failure to perform even the most basic duties of a lodge. For example, too many lodges have officers who simply do not know the few lines of ritual necessary to open or close a lodge. Too many Senior Deacons are incapable of properly introducing and receiving Grand Lodge officers or visitors. Too many lodges must call on outside degree teams to confer degrees on candidates or to conduct Masonic funerals.

Before we attempt to teach any advanced concepts in Freemasonry, we should begin with the basics of lodge operation. If you are a young Mason and you seek Masonic education in your lodge, then be mindful of what you see in the lodge, and do not attempt to take on too much too quickly.

Another area, or subject, for basic Masonic education would be Masonic titles that are used for various lodge and Grand Lodge officers. Without question, the Senior Deacon should know the proper title for someone that he is introducing. Nerves can come into play, and anyone can make a mistake with a title or any other aspect of ritual. But if a Senior Deacon simply cannot introduce a District Deputy Grand Master or any Grand Lodge officer with the proper titles repeatedly then the lodge needs a new Senior Deacon. Period. The lodge is doing a disservice to itself, the Grand Lodge, and everyone involved if they allow someone who cannot, or does not, perform his duties to remain in office.

We must have individuals who have both the desire to learn and the ability to perform their duties. But the Senior Deacon is not the only one who needs to learn how to properly address various lodge and Grand Lodge officers. All members of the lodge need to learn the basics of Masonic courtesy when addressing Masons in lodge. This can sometimes be a tricky matter and discretion often needs to be employed with titles. For example, most jurisdictions address a Grand Master as *Most Worshipful Brother*. This form of address, in most jurisdictions, will remain after the Grand Master leaves office — but not always. Check titles!

If you personally know and are good friends with a Mason who advances through the chairs to the office of Grand Master, how you address him depends on the setting. In private conversation, it's perfectly acceptable to address him by his first name if you know him well. For many, not to do so would seem odd and almost an insult. However, he should be addressed as *Most Worshipful Brother* when speaking of him, or to him, in the lodge. The same is true for any title that is used in a craft lodge setting. When the lodge is at labor, each brother should be addressed either directly, or when speaking of him, with the proper title that they have earned. Even if the brother is your best friend, or family member, they should be addressed in lodge by their Masonic title.

When communicating to Masons, the context of the communication should be considered. Today we live in a world where communication is far more informal than in the past. A text message may be void of everything except the message itself. But when addressing a Mason in any formal mail, including newsletters and other publications, proper Masonic titles should be given.

If a brother has earned the title of Worshipful Brother, or Right Worshipful Brother, Most Worshipful Brother, or any other title given to them in a craft lodge or by the Grand Lodge, the complete and correct title should be used in any formal communication. If you don't know the complete and correct title of someone, ask a knowledgeable brother before you send out a communication.

If you are yourself addressed in a formal setting, such as a lodge, by an incorrect title, it does no one any favors if you allow the error to slide by simply because you don't want to make a "big deal" out of it. I don't mean that you should correct someone in the middle of a ceremony, but you should inform the one who made the error of their mistake in private after the ceremony is over. An error made concerning a proper title is not something that should require a chewing out or anything more than a friendly comment giving them the correct title for the future.

These are the types of education programs that should be started in a lodge that has been without any Masonic education for a number of years. The basics of opening and closing, receiving visitors, funerals, and proper titles are a few of the basic subjects that should be given with Masonic education programs.

Personally, these are the areas where I see most errors being made by lodges. Working with these subjects first can provide useful and appreciated Masonic education programs for any lodge. Once a lodge is completely competent in all areas of basic operation, then, step-by-step, more of the advanced subjects can be covered. It is not by coincidence that Freemasonry teaches by degrees, and we should use this practice and teaching philosophy with all Masonic education programs.

Ostracizing "the Other"

Human nature is such that it always seems easier to criticize, blame and attack the other guy or a group *over there* rather than ourselves or one from our group. All of our problems *must* be because of those other guys and if they would only be like us, or join us, then all of our problems would certainly go away. Throughout history we can point to numerous examples of how one group would minimize, dehumanize, and place all blame for problems on another group rather than just accept that we can all be different and work together. Maybe we find it easier to place blame rather than accept responsibility and deal with issues ourselves. But why?

Masonry provides a blueprint in its teachings that, if applied, can help us improve ourselves. Our goal is often stated that we take good men and make them better. But, if we achieve that goal, why do we have disagreements and even harsh conflicts between Masons? I believe that an answer might be found in the early days of Masonry in the United States. A flaw may exist in our initial U.S. Masonic design.

In the early days of U.S. Masonry, there was a desire for each Grand Lodge to be sovereign, but for the Masonic experience in one place to be very similar to other places. There was a desire for one ritual (Preston-Webb) and one language (English). There was a desire for all lodges and all Masons to be the same—on the level. The problem is that we are not all the same. We have different likes, dislikes, abilities, dreams, and goals. We don't look or act the same. So, if we are supposed to all be alike, but we are different, then it follows that *different* may also be a judgement (better or worse). Insecurities can then creep in suggesting that *the other* thinks of himself as (or, worse yet, is) better than us! That does not make us feel good, and it does not matter if such evaluations are sound or logical. If we feel something, we feel it. We then need rank, position, degrees, and authority to make us feel better and superior to *the other* who is different than us. We would also need to hold down the troublemakers so that they are put in their perceived place. Ostracizing *the other* allows us to preserve any illusions that we may have of ourselves and relieves us of any guilt in our actions against *the other*. The need for all this extra effort seems to be a valid reason to dislike *the other*.

When differences are acknowledged as the norm, our expectations allow for these differences. It is okay if some can sing beautifully while we can't carry a tune in a bucket. Or some are better at math or art. When we recognize that we are all different, then our own personal talents (maybe very different than the talents of others) are allowed to develop with no judgement or envy concerning another's talent. We can enjoy each other and the variety of experiences. The Masonic goal of making ourselves better puts us in sole competition with ourselves and not our neighbor. There is no longer a need to focus on what *the other* can or cannot do. We judge our own work, not the work of anyone else.

Perhaps Masonry in the U.S. would benefit by taking a close look at Masonry around the world. We can find diversity in ritual, language, and practices. Differences are recognized and embraced. Where you see variety in the Masonic experience, you see Masonic growth. If we are stuck in "the way it has always been done" mindset, then we must realize that we are not speaking of the whole of Masonry around the world. We are speaking only of *our* Masonry, not *the others*.

Few enjoy being forced into something undesired. If I enjoy strawberry ice cream, why should I be forced into eating rocky road? If we desire that all our lodges be alike, then we need to recognize that others may desire their lodges to be a little different, and that is okay. If the ritual is different (but delivers the Hiramic Legend), or if they all wear tuxes (or, overalls), or if they do, or do not, read their minutes, it is okay. We need to recognize that we do not all need to be in lock-step with each other. We should spend our time working on the improvement of ourselves rather than on finding fault with *the other*.

Innovations in Freemasonry

Recently, I saw a debate between two Masons. The debate concerned the subject of lodges doing business on the Entered Apprentice degree. Not too long ago, I did a video on this very subject. But that subject is not the point of this piece. It was something else that came out of the debate.

While the brother advocating for lodges to work on the Entered Apprentice degree made his case, the brother arguing against it did not say anything other than give his reason as to why he believes it cannot be allowed. He said that conducting business on the Entered Apprentice degree is not allowed because it would be an *innovation* in Masonry, which he said is simply not allowed. I've heard this before in a few different places.

The brother arguing against the change made two mistakes in his position — one was a historical error, and the other was an error of definition. The historical error was in believing that working on the Entered Apprentice degree was something new. Far too many times, we see something as *having always been that way*. We usually see it as *having always existed* if it has been unchanged for as long as we have been Masons, or those before us.

The fact is that prior to the early/mid 1800s, Masonic lodges in the US worked on the Entered Apprentice degree. This was the norm for Masonic lodges. It was only *after* that time that US lodges made the change to working on the Master Mason degree. This change was likely made in large part because of the strong anti-Masonic activities that were taking place mainly in the New England states during the early to mid-1800s. It seems there was a feeling that the business of a lodge could only be entrusted to one who had completed all of the Craft Lodge degrees.

Regardless of the actual reason, the business of a lodge made the switch from being conducted on the Entered Apprentice degree to the Master Mason degree beginning in the early 1800s. By the mid-1800s, all US Grand Lodges had made the switch to conducting lodge business meetings to the Master Mason degree.

So, if making a change in the degree which a lodge conducts its business is an innovation then that innovation was made when lodges switched to conducting business on the Master Mason degree. But what is an innovation? The idea that Masonry cannot make innovations is nonsense. It's done every year at Grand Lodge sessions.

Every time the Grand Lodge approves a resolution, or a lodge amends its bylaws, that's an innovation. When it is said that no Mason or body of Masons can make innovations in Masonry, it is clearly implied that this means *unauthorized* innovations.

For example, if a Mason decides on his own that he can amend his obligations to ones that better suit him, well he's wrong. That would be an *unauthorized* innovation. No Mason on his own is authorized to make changes in any aspect of our ritual, or laws, without following proper channels.

Likewise, if someone stands up during a lodge meeting and suggests that he wants to change the bylaws and then the lodge immediately votes to make these changes, well, that's usually not allowed in a lodge setting. Changing a lodge's bylaws, and how to do it, is usually clearly spelled out in the Grand Lodge law books. It is usually necessary for all the members of the lodge to be given proper notice of a proposed change so they will have the opportunity of discussing and voting on the change.

It was never meant that innovations are *never* allowed in Masonry. It simply meant that *improper* innovations are not allowed. Lodges and Grand Lodges have defined methods of making changes, or innovations, in their laws and practices. When the proper methods are followed, innovations can, and are, made.

When you wonder about any aspect of Freemasonry, ask questions. If you receive answers that seem questionable, continue asking and seeking. Look in your book of law. Ask your Grand Secretaries office. Ask your DDGM or a Mason you know to be knowledgeable. Do a little digging. Answers can always be found with a little work.

Shadows of Our Masonic Past

Human beings are complex creatures, and we have certain needs. Some of these needs are physical and others emotional. Physical needs might be something along the lines of food or shelter, but we also have these other inner demands. One of the most fundamental is the need to understand ourselves. We want to understand who we are, what we are, and where we came from. If we don't have a complete understanding of ourselves, then we are left with questions that poke at us insistently. The lack of a proper and complete understanding of ourselves can even deny us the peace of mind that we all crave.

Because Freemasonry is such an important part of the lives of so many Freemasons, it faces the same problems of identity as individuals face. We, as an organization, have the need to understand Freemasonry, who we are as Freemasons, and the basic questions of our origin. The problem that we face is that so much of our early Masonic history is either incorrectly written, misunderstood, or not available at all to us. This creates large gaps in what we understand about ourselves and prevents us from properly understanding the nature of early Freemasonry.

I believe that we might begin to understand Freemasonry a bit more if we look at it through different stages or levels. The first that we might study is our own personal level. This would be Masonry that we have personally experienced — our own lodge or lodges that we have visited. This would be our own first-hand experience with Freemasonry. The next level is the Masonry which was explained to us by Masons we know. It could be the Masonry currently existing in a different city, state, or country. We learn of this extended Masonry through interaction with those who have experienced it, but without our having visited these lodges ourselves. It could also be talking with much older Masons who will speak of Masonry that, maybe, was a bit different prior to our joining. This would give us a window into Masonry from the recent past. We can take this leveling back through books to the earliest times of Freemasonry. Certainly, Masonry as practiced in the 1700's was different than the 1800's. Likewise, Masonry during most of the 1900's was different than it is today. And by that, I mean the entire Masonic experience or what each Mason would see and hear in a lodge. We can also look at the Masonry practiced in different areas and jurisdictions. Many have different customs and practices. The whole point is that there is no such thing as one type of Masonry. Masonry has existed in different forms and practices since its very early days. Certainly, if we were able to go back in time and visit a lodge from say the early 1700's, the Masonic experience from that time would be dramatically different than today's Masonic experience.

A common thread that links all of Masonry is that all Masonic bodies have some sort of governing regulations. It may be, or may have been, called constitutions, or bylaws, or any one of a number of terms. There is always some guiding organized system for the operation of lodges and bodies. The problem that we often run into is that we call ourselves "Speculative Freemasonry" but link ourselves historically to the old Operative Freemasons. We even claim the Operatives as our forefathers. Maybe this is true, or maybe not. But we quickly run into trouble when we try to get a firm grasp on the rules and regulations of the old Operative lodges. Now, early on in Speculative Masonry they came up with a term known as "landmarks" which habitually seems to be alluded to as the *guiding rules* governing Operative Freemasonry. The clear suggestion is that these landmarks were the rules and guide for the Operatives. Today, however, we realize that there is a major problem when we look at something so historically elusive as the operation of the old Operative guilds and try to apply these landmarks to them.

The problem that we run into with the concept of landmarks is that there is a suggestion that there was only one set of landmarks (or rules) and that they applied universally to all the old Operative lodges. But we are today beginning to see that these Operative lodges worked, to some degree, along the same lines as Grand Lodges today. By that I mean that each one seems to have their own set of governing rules and regulations. Really, each had their own "landmarks." To think that any two old Operative lodges would have had the exact same set of rules or laws is the same as thinking that any two Grand Lodges today have the same set of rules and regulations. Of course, there would have been similar basic requirements.

If we take a look at the old Operative Masons, these were individuals who were highly skilled craftsmen. They were responsible for building some of the magnificent structures in Europe. They were hard working men. They had certain requirements, including moral requirements. They did not want someone who would join their company who they could not trust. They would, for the most part, select and only consider men for most all their positions. The reason was simple. They wanted someone who they felt could do hard, physical work. A young man was also not considered nor was an old man. They would not select someone who had a physical handicap because they felt this would prevent them from doing the hard, manual labor that would be required of them. So, some of what we look at as "landmarks" were only business practices that were common for the time. But, when we talk about things like the "25 Landmarks" by Albert Mackey, we must realize that these so-called "landmarks" were created at a much later date and then applied to the old Operatives. When we talk today about the "Landmarks of Freemasonry," we are really talking about what each and every Grand Lodge has decided are rules and laws for their jurisdiction. The fact is that the "landmarks" are more opinion than fact. Each Grand Lodge decides for itself the definition of a "landmark." As such, the landmarks of the Grand Lodges are anything but carbon copies of each other.

So, while the list of so-called landmarks can vary from jurisdiction to jurisdiction, and while there is no one single list of Ancient Landmarks that is accepted as the definitive landmarks by all jurisdictions, there are certain elements within the lists which have historically been generally accepted over the years. These normally apply to one's fitness for joining Freemasonry. These requirements have pretty much remained the standard until recent years. Over the last years, we have had a number of jurisdictions review several of the so-called "landmarks" and realized that there was no need for one to do hard, manual labor in our Freemasonry. We are not Operative Masons and do not construct buildings. It was realized that the "landmark" prohibiting one from joining if they had any physical handicap was not necessary for our Speculative Freemasonry. So, we have overturned one of the old requirements or landmarks based on a reevaluation of who and what we are as Freemasons. While it is understood that one may have needed to be in perfect physical shape for the old Operative Masons, we are Speculative Masons, and such requirements are not necessary for our work of building the internal self. Of course, this gives us cause to question if other aspects or requirements offered in the landmarks are also unnecessary today or if some of these old landmarks have already changed with us not being completely aware of the changes.

There is another aspect of the landmarks, and the concept of "fitness to join" which has changed or, maybe, our understanding of it has changed. I'm not exactly sure what has caused this change of understanding, but I wanted to talk a little about it. It has to do with a particular word which is "freeborn." Now, the idea is that one who is not "freeborn" (or, *free born*) is not eligible to join Freemasonry. In my early days as a Mason, I was told that this means that a slave cannot join. What I find interesting is the spelling of this word. I see this word spelled in many of the early documents as *free borne*. Interestingly, when you spell the word in that manner, it takes on a new meaning. In the English of the 1400's, 1500's or even later, *free born* simply means one who is born free or not born into slavery. But *free borne* is understood differently when we look at the English language of the time when Operative Masonry was declining and with the birth of Speculative

Freemasonry. The time frame would be late 1600's and early 1700's. The word *borne* was understood to mean "to carry." With that understanding of the word, the term *free borne* would mean that one was free to carry something. In the Masonic context, one requirement for joining Masonry was if one were free to pick up his tools and carry them to wherever the work was located. In other words, one could not be a Freemason if he were a slave. It was necessary that a Freemason be able to freely travel to wherever the work was located. But this is quite a different understanding than one who is born free, or not born into slavery. By the understanding of the older spelling of the word, if someone had at some time been a slave, that would not necessarily deprive him of being a Freemason if he were not a slave when he was accepted. If, when you became a Freemason, you were not a slave and free to be able to pick up your tools to travel wherever needed, then there should be no problem.

It is, frankly, impossible to believe that racism did not come into play with our understanding of this "landmark" especially in the United States and especially prior to and following the time of the Civil War. It would be naive or deceptive to suggest that racism did not have a role in the whole of American Freemasonry. *Freeborn* would take on a meaning that if one was born into slavery then they would not be eligible to join at any time during their life, even if later freed. Let's say someone was born into slavery prior to the Civil War and then freed following the war; they would still not be eligible to join after they were freed by this understanding of the word. I've also heard arguments that the word *freeborn* applied to not only you, but your parents, grandparents, and for as many generations back (and forward) as one chose.

So, it's hard to understand how this landmark interpretation could not be born out of racism. What seems to be needed is to understand the nature of the old Operatives and how they conducted business. For them, freedom was everything. Freedom was necessary for their work. If they were offered a job, it could be anywhere. It was necessary that all of the workers be able to pick up and travel to wherever the job was located. They had to be free, not a slave or a bondsman or anyone who was required to remain in one area. But, it is quite a different meaning if *freeborn* is understood that one would never be able to join, if they had at any time been a slave – or, someone in their family had been a slave. Simply put, why in the world would the old Operatives care if a good worker was at some time a slave or some member of his family was at some time a slave? If they were a good worker and not a slave *at that time*, then that is all they would have logically cared about.

Now, there is another of the "landmarks" that I believe I would be insincere if I did not mention. That would be the landmark requiring Speculative Freemasonry to be limited to males only. I'm not going to do more than mention it in this paper as later in this book another paper is offered (*Women and Freemasonry*) where we will discuss the existence, history, and development of women in Masonry.

When we talk about the Ancient Landmarks or the Landmarks of Freemasonry, we are talking about a collection of old manuscript documents that pertain to the old Operative Freemasons. From these ancient documents we have been able to gather a general idea of how the old Operatives organized themselves and more information on the operatives themselves. We've taken the information continued in these old documents and gathered them together calling them the *Ancient Landmarks*. Whether they were actually used by the old Operatives or if they were widely used, we are not sure. But we have claimed them as what we believe to have been the rules or laws of the old Operatives. Once we moved into the era of Speculative Masonry, we developed a new set of rules or laws which we called *Constitutions*. These constitutions were built upon what we understand of the old rules and laws of the Operatives. With that, we were able to claim a transition from Operative Freemasonry to Speculative Freemasonry. The key is that most of what we have in this collection is speculation. What we can prove as fact is very little.

In 2006, I had the privilege of editing a book titled, *Masonic Enlightenment.*[1] In that book, Lionel Vibert offers a paper titled "Anderson's Constitutions of 1723." Bro. Vibert makes a very important point very early in the paper, and it is one that we should keep in mind when we look at the period around the beginning of Speculative Freemasonry. As Bro. Vibert points out, while 1717 is the date that is normally given as to when the first Grand Lodge of London was created or the first Grand Lodge of Speculative Freemasonry, he points out rather clearly that there is no information provided, or recorded, coming from this new Grand Lodge for the first few years. We just don't exactly know what happened during those early years. The first real look we have at the early years was not until 1738, when James Anderson provides a history which is, at best, questionable concerning the early years of this new Speculative Grand Lodge. It's important to look at these early years and look at what we do know of the old Operative Freemasons.

When we take a look at the old system of Operative Freemasonry and look at the time around when we find the birth of Speculative Freemasonry, we need to take another look at the Operative Masons themselves to try and understand who and what they were. Certainly, the Operatives were highly skilled craftsmen. But there is another aspect that we need to focus on to get a better picture of what was taking place and why some felt that Speculative Freemasonry was very desirable. You see, if you go back to the period a little before and a little after the Middle Ages, some of the most educated individuals were the merchants. The merchants would travel from area to area to sell whatever items they were selling. It was this travelling from different areas that gave the merchants experience and knowledge of new events happening, customs, discoveries, or just general news from different areas. Individuals who did not travel far from their village valued the knowledge, news, and information possessed by these merchants. The same was true of the old Operative Masons. The operatives would travel from place to place and exchange ideas, news, and information with the locals wherever their work would take them. It was not just the skill of the Operatives in building, which was of course of great value in itself, but the individual Operatives who brought news, information, new ideas, and interesting stories and discussion with the locals that was of great value. They were respected and valued visitors to the lands they travelled. When the Operatives came to town, it was always a major event.

Notes:

1. Michael R. Poll, ed., *Masonic Enlightenment* (New Orleans, LA: Cornerstone Book Publishers, 2006)

Freemasonry and Social Media

In the very early days of the Internet, pretty much everything was new and amazing. I remember going to RadioShack and buying a Tandy computer. It was a dial-up Internet connection through CompuServe. This meant that to connect to the Internet I had to unplug my phone, and by that, I mean my landline phone. I wouldn't have a cell phone for a good number of years to come. I would connect the land line phone to my computer. I would then dial-up CompuServe on the computer and connect to the Internet. It was an incredible feeling to discover the various forums on CompuServe. The world instantly became much smaller.

I joined CompuServe sometime in the mid to late 1980s, and there was already a thriving community there with forums on pretty much every subject. I decided to look up Freemasonry and discovered that there was a forum called the CompuServe Masonry Forum. I joined it. It was more than I had expected.

Just sitting at my desk in front of my computer, I was able to speak, at least through a keyboard, with Masons in pretty much all corners of the world. This was an impossible thing to do before the internet. The only way to do such a thing prior to the internet was to physically travel all over the world. Most of us could not do this.

I remained on this forum until it closed sometime, I believe, not too long after 2000. I even became a moderator for the forum. It was called a Systems Operator, or Sysop for short. During this time, most Grand Lodges had no opinion whatsoever about these forums. I'm not sure if most of the Grand Lodges were even aware of them at that time. But a couple were and had rather strong opinions.

For example, the United Grand Lodge of England, for a time, would not allow its members to participate in any online forum at all. It seems to have been felt that the opportunity to violate obligations was too great. This was, however, short-lived as it was most likely realized that the Internet was here to stay, and it was having a growing influence on all of society.

By the mid-to late 90s, the internet was a major part of the lives of many people as well as many businesses and organizations. Information and business websites began appearing. Slowly, Masonic lodges began developing their own websites and following that, at a slower pace, Grand Lodges began developing their own pages on the internet. Content was always a matter of debate.

It seems that there was always a discussion as to the purpose of the website and how much information should be put out there for the public. During this same time, membership in many Grand Lodges was diminishing, and these websites were seen as a promising tool for building membership. The problem faced by many jurisdictions was the lack of skill of those in charge of building websites. Young internet savvy Masons were often contracted to take care of the website creation for lodges and Grand Lodges.

In the US, it soon became apparent that abuse could take place on the internet. There were various suspensions due to what was felt to be unMasonic conduct on various online forums, e-mail lists, and website discussion boards. Some Grand Lodges felt the need to create rules and regulations governing conduct by Masons on the Internet. But, before too long, every lodge, district lodge, association and pretty much every organization within Masonry not only had websites, but Facebook pages, twitter accounts, and who knows how many other social media outlets.

It's clear as to the dangers of the internet or any on-line forum. Simply put, an on-line forum is not a tiled lodge. Nothing on the internet is tiled. Period. I've seen some on-line forums claim to be restricted to only "regular" Masons with copies of dues cards required for admission. It's nonsense. There is no such thing as a tiled on-line forum or anywhere on the internet that is free from being hacked.

I was a member of one such on-line forum when the moderator seemed to be posting something strange only to learn that a former member of the forum had hacked into the moderator's account and posted as if it were the moderator. A lodge is a lodge, and any other place is not a lodge. I post nothing anywhere on-line or in any video that I would not be willing to post in a public newspaper.

If you are uncomfortable with what you post being shared all over the world, then don't post it anywhere on-line.

It's pretty much as simple as that. But this should be common sense and is covered in most of the rules Grand Lodges have published on internet use. Still, these are the things not to do.

Let's look at a few things that a lodge might want to do to make the best use of the internet. Let's start with what should be obvious … Masonry does not, or should not, solicit members. We should not use any aspect of social media to overtly try to bring in new members. I know that some jurisdictions have become lax in that old provision, but in my opinion, that does not help Freemasonry.

Freemasonry is set apart from clubs and other organizations because we initiate our candidates. One aspect of a valid initiation is that a candidate must have the desire to be initiated. This is why so many of the old Masonic texts stress that the candidate comes to the lodge of his own free will and accord. If he is invited to join or worse yet, pressured to join, then the benefits of initiation may well be lost. If we do not realize or believe that initiation has any benefits to the candidate, then the whole of Freemasonry is reduced to a simple club.

If transforming into a club is where we wish to go, then we should stop all the needless initiations, investigation committees, and all other non-club aspects of Masonry and just cash the checks and let everyone in. But … not inviting someone to join is different from making your lodge's existence known and clearing up misconceptions of Freemasonry.

One with a true desire to join, but who has no idea as to who to reach out to, is denied membership needlessly. By making events of the lodge known by the proper use of social media not only informs and inspires lodge members to participate, but also makes the lodge visible to those with a desire to join. In addition, in those jurisdictions where plural memberships are allowed, there is nothing at all wrong with a lodge announcing that it is accepting plural members. In these cases, we're not talking about initiating candidates, but a lodge taking in as plural members Masons from other lodges.

Social media can also be used to better spread information about a lodge such as new lodge offices following the annual elections, a lodge moving from one location to another, or other notable changes or events in the lodge. Banquets and other public events taking place in the lodge can be announced on websites or social media creating positive publicity for the event, the lodge, and the whole of Freemasonry.

When properly used, social media can be an excellent tool for Masonic education as well as presenting Masonry to the public in the correct light. With just a little bit of creativity and planning, social media can be used to build interest in lodge meetings by announcing planned meals, events, schedule degrees, or plan visits by Grand Lodge officers or any other dignitaries.

If all social media is used for is the announcement of the lodge name, address, and meeting dates then great opportunities are missed. I also suggest that all media, from websites to Facebook pages, twitter or any other media outlets that are used be updated and used regularly. To visit a website that is obviously unattended and possibly even lists officers from several years past is worse than useless. It presents an image of a lodge that is sloppy, disinterested, and lacking anything of value.

By using all forms of social media on a regular basis, a lodge shows that it is active, interested in its members, and working to be the best that it can be. Visiting other lodge websites or social media outlets can give you ideas on what you can do for your lodge.

Since most cell phones today have quality cameras included, there is no excuse for not taking lots of photos of any events in your lodge and posting them on your social media. Photos of happy people gathering for some event and obviously having a good time is infectious. Avoid photos showing many empty chairs, bad shots of anyone, or photos showing anyone having less than a good time. By taking many photos, it is easier to select the more positive ones to promote your event.

By using social media as a tool, your lodge can benefit greatly. All you need to do is give it a little planning, research into what others are doing and a bit of organization. The effective use of social media is one more step towards a successful lodge.

Who Can be a Scottish Rite Mason?

You know, sometimes I get emails that I can quickly answer. Sometimes I get emails that I can't answer at all. But then, sometimes I get emails that make me stop and think. Even if I know that it's a simple question, sometimes I see more in it if I look at the question from, maybe, around the corner. Such was the case with one email I received. It was a simple, straightforward question.

I was asked, "Who can be a Scottish Rite Mason?" The brother didn't give me a lot of information about himself, but he did say that he was Senior Deacon of his lodge and that he had been a Mason "for a few years." The easy answer is that he should be able to go and pay the secretary of his Valley a visit. There, he could pick up an application and learn any details of his Valley. I assumed that this was what he was asking and sent him this information. He sent me back a thank you note. But I continued to look at the question and I realized that depending on who was asking it, that question could mean a lot of different things.

For example, what is someone's understanding of "Scottish Rite Mason?" Also, does he mean, "who can" or "who should"? I'd like to dissect this question a bit and try to examine it from a few different sides. Also at the beginning, I'd like to add a disclaimer of sorts. The Ancient and Accepted Scottish Rite is a 33-degree system. It begins in the Entered Apprentice degree and concludes with the degree of Sovereign Grand Inspector General.

Now, this does not mean that every Scottish Rite body confers every degree of the Scottish Rite. Different degrees are conferred by different bodies. In addition, some Supreme Councils have modified the degrees worked in their bodies. But, regardless of any of this, the system is a 33 degree system. For the benefit of this discussion, however, I will use the term *Scottish Rite* to refer to the fourth degree and above.

I remember a good many years ago when I first joined the Valley of New Orleans, I was eager to participate in every way that I could. Learning the ritual was rather easy for me, and it was something in which I excelled. This somewhat transferred over to the Scottish Rite. I began taking part in a number of the class degrees, some of them as part of the permanent degree teams and some filling in as needed.

In truth, the degrees of the Scottish Rite were exactly what I was looking for out of Masonry. I could see in the Scottish Rite a profound philosophy, a system of moral teachings of integrity, honor, justice, and so much more. I spent a good bit of time trying to read up on as much as I could on the philosophy of the Scottish Rite. I would also try to talk with as many of the older members as possible, trying to pick their brains. But then one of them told me something that made me stop and wonder.

We were talking about the philosophy of the Scottish Rite, and he was the first one, at least, the first that I remember, who said that the Scottish Rite was the *college of Freemasonry*. I'm sure the term had been used many times before, but this was the first time I had heard it. I understood what he meant and did agree with him. But then he added something that took me by surprise. He said that it was his opinion that no one should be allowed to join the Scottish Rite unless they had a college degree. He said that the lessons of the Scottish Rite were of such a nature that they could not be understood by "uneducated individuals." I did a lot of thinking about that statement. It calls for a clear judgment of others.

I began thinking about my grandfather. He was the reason that I joined Freemasonry. He came to the United States when he was 15 years old. He was from what was then Yugoslavia and is now Croatia. He barely had a grammar school education, and yet he could speak seven languages. The books that he had around his house were some of the deepest philosophical books ever in print. He was also a member of the New Orleans Valley. I could think of no one more worthy, eligible, and a true Scottish Rite Mason than my grandfather. So, why would this Mason say such a thing? It was at this time that I realized that many see the Scottish Rite from different perspectives.

I very much agree that not everyone, and that includes not every Mason, should be a Scottish Rite Mason. This is not a slight against any Mason, but just an evaluation of both Freemasonry and the Scottish Rite. I'm not passing judgment on anyone, only observing that it may not be of the liking to all. I don't assume that everyone likes the same flavor of ice cream that I like, nor do I assume that my taste in Masonry is the same as everyone else. But I do not, at all, believe that a degree from a college is any sort of valid appraisal of the worthiness of one to join the Scottish Rite.

I do understand the concept that some jurisdictions have of the Scottish Rite being more exclusive. In some jurisdictions one does not *join* the Scottish Rite, they must be invited. If no invitation comes, then they will never receive the fourth degree in the Scottish Rite. The problem is that all of this can possibly take on a sinister undertone if it is received, or practiced, without the highest of moral integrity. The truth is that far too many view the Scottish Rite as a club. Maybe they use it to gain honors, status, or power. Maybe they just enjoy the company of those Masons who belong to different lodges and who they may only see once a month at a consistory meeting. Regardless, they don't choose to use the deep lessons in the rituals of the Scottish Rite as anything more than necessary ritual plays that one witnesses, or in which one participates, to join.

I'm going to set these brothers aside for the balance of this discussion and focus only on those who see the Scottish Rite as a system of profound philosophy and use it *as* a college of Freemasonry — in other words, a system designed to gain personal enlightenment. If you have a desire to learn more of the deeper aspects of Freemasonry, then the Scottish Rite is for you. You will need to ignore those who use the system only as a tool to feed their ego by means of obtaining honors or degrees. You should focus only on the Scottish Rite ritual and philosophy. But, by doing so you can uncover a profound system of Masonic education. The deeper aspects of integrity, honor, responsibility, justice and so much more will be explained in a way that many will never understand. Yes, the Knights Templar as well as other knightly orders are highlighted in the ritual of the Scottish Rite. They have been there since the earliest times of the Rite.

Once at a Scottish Rite reunion I overheard someone going from table to table where the candidates were sitting, telling them that to *complete* the Scottish Rite degrees they would need to petition the York Rite. In the United States, this is *absolutely* 100% false. Both the York Rite and the Scottish Rite are beautiful complete systems. Neither depends on the other to complete either system. Many Masons belong to both Rites, and this is great. But no one should be tricked into believing that either system depends on the other for complete understanding of their own system. It's just not true. When you begin your study of the Ancient and Accepted Scottish Rite don't forget to study the craft degrees of that system.

Without an understanding of the Scottish Rite craft lodges, the foundation of the Scottish Rite is taken away leaving you with an incomplete understanding of this profound system. So, if you are looking for the deeper aspects of Freemasonry, the Scottish Rite is something you should join. It's as simple as that.

By just scratching the surface of the Scottish Rite's philosophy and teachings, you'll find alchemy, the hermetic arts, the honor codes of the Knights Templar, and so very much more that will provide you with the very reasons as to why you join Freemasonry in the first place. The Scottish Rite might be viewed by the unenlightened as a place where you can become a "big shot." Sure, if that's what you need.

But for those who truly understand the meaning of enlightenment, they will find in the Scottish Rite a rich and meaningful path to what they are seeking. If this applies to you, then you can and really should join the Scottish Rite.

Women and Freemasonry

It has been my experience that there are a few hot button topics within Freemasonry. These would be subjects that quickly generate a good bit of emotion with many Masons. One such subject is if the Volume of Sacred Law can be removed from the altar of the lodge and the lodge remain regular. Most say no. Another subject is if women can become Freemasons.

The point of this paper is certainly not to stir up emotions or to do anything other than a simple examination of the subject. I will take no position at all regarding the subject of women in Freemasonry. The only position that I will take is that I will uphold the laws of my jurisdiction.

One of the so-called landmarks that is accepted by every recognized Grand Lodge of which I am familiar is that a woman cannot become a Freemason. What I have not seen answered in any satisfactory manner is the simple question of why it is not possible. The most often answer given is that it is prohibited in the Landmarks. But is it?

When we look at the Operative Freemasons, it is obvious that a woman might not be able to do the physical labor that was so often demanded of the Operatives. But is a ban on women an actual landmark? And if so, is it one that is valid today?

I know several lodges who have admitted candidates who have physical handicaps. The reason for doing so is simple; we are not Operative Freemasons. We do not need to be sound of body to improve ourselves with the teachings of Speculative Freemasonry.

If this landmark regarding physical fitness can be reasonably seen as unnecessary today for Speculative Freemasonry, then why is the landmark prohibiting women viewed as unchangeable? It's true that no one is doing hard physical work in Speculative Freemasonry. So why is it impossible for a woman to be a Freemason?

Maybe before we get into possible questions of why not, we need to look a bit at how we are set up as Grand Lodges. Each Grand Lodge is sovereign and independent. Yet in the United States, the sovereign and independent Grand Lodges have something of an organized understanding. While it is understood that Grand Lodges have their own rules and regulations, there are certain aspects of the operation of the Grand Lodges that are expected to be common and shared. For example, any Grand Lodge that would remove the Volume of Sacred Law from the altar of their lodges would be viewed as irregular and the balance of US Grand Lodges would most likely break fraternal relations with them. The same is true for admitting women into lodges. We may not be exactly sure as to why this is true, but I can assure you it is true.

I also believe that it is true to say that in many US Grand Lodges the personality of the Grand Master can play a good part in determining how conservative or liberal the tone of the Grand Lodge will be during his term in office. I have seen some cases where to even suggest that female Masonry exists is deemed acceptable grounds for Masonic discipline by some Grand Masters.

Some years back, I was told by a Mason, and in all sincerity, that the entire concept of female Masonry was the creation of the anti-Masons. I was told that there was no such thing, at all, as female Masons and photographs and reports of them were entirely made up. The entire subject of female Masonry is for some reason and many times very much like walking on thin ice. Simply discussing the subject can sometimes result in trouble.

I know of one case where a Mason was told point blank that if he even speaks to a female Mason, that is grounds for Masonic discipline. He was told that the same is true for any Mason who is not in fraternal relations with his Grand Lodge. When asked about a situation where one was working with someone who was a member of a lodge not recognized by their jurisdiction, the Mason was told that he should find another job. I do not believe that these sorts of extreme examples are either logical or display proper understanding of Masonic obligations.

The Operative Masonic lodges were not civic or social clubs. They were places of business. The Operative Masons accepted construction jobs, travelled from area to area, and worked sometimes hard, difficult jobs as a profession. This was their livelihood and how they fed themselves and their families. Their reputation was everything for them. With a good reputation, they could continue to secure work. A bad reputation could mean that they did not work. If they did not work, they did not eat.

An Operative Lodge could not afford to have anyone as a member who could not do the work or was any sort of issue that could damage their reputation. A woman was not considered, on the average, capable of doing the hard manual labor that was expected of the Operative Masons. They were put in the same category as young boys, old men, or those with physical handicaps. They simply needed to be sure that the ones accepted into their lodges could do the work that was necessary.

But there could be another reason, at that time, a woman may not be considered acceptable to become an Operative Freemason. During the medieval times, as well as other times, a woman was considered the property of her father until marriage. Upon marriage, a woman became the property of her husband. A woman, during many times in history, had no legal standing, and shared the status of her father or husband. As such, a woman would not be free to pick up and travel with an Operative Lodge if work was needed in another land. So, if we step back and objectively look at the situation, it does seem logical that if a woman had travel or physical restrictions, they would not be a good candidate for an Operative Freemason. But also, objectively, it would *not* seem that a woman would be unable to provide *any* service to an Operative Lodge. In fact, some of the early accounts of Operative Masonry offer hints that women *could have* served in Operative Lodges.

In two sections of the *Regius Manuscript*, a poem dated about 1390, and considered the oldest known document concerning Operative Freemasonry, there seems to be mentioned of women as Operative Masons. In lines 41 and 42 and in Article 10, it mentions "sisters and brothers" in reference to an Operative Lodge.

Could this mean that women *may* have performed some duties for an Operative Lodge? It's certainly not definitive, but let's think about it. Not every duty performed in the construction of a building was necessarily hard physical labor. Artisans were often employed to carve the beautiful woodwork on staircases, around doorways, and other areas. A woman who was a gifted artist could certainly do this type of work.

I have read several unconfirmed reports where such women were the daughters or wives of Operative Freemasons. In such cases, they would be free to travel with the lodge, along with their father or husband. Under these conditions, it seems reasonable that a woman *could* serve as an Operative Freemason. Logic would dictate that this would not be the norm, but it would be possible. After all, the lodge was a place of business, and their main concern was providing their customers with excellent craftsmen capable of doing the work necessary and constructing a beautiful building. If a woman were capable of doing any aspect of this work and doing so at a quality equal to or surpassing a male, then why would the lodge not hire her? It would be bad for business for them *not* to do so.

We have very little concrete information concerning the makeup of the members of any Operative Lodge, much less all of them. The Operative Lodges, responsible for constructing so many of the beautiful structures and cathedrals in Europe for some 400 to 500 years, employed countless laborers, artisans, designers, and other workers necessary for these building jobs. With the variety of different work that was necessary, it would seem illogical that *no woman* would ever qualify for *any* of the positions during all those years.

It would also seem logical that given the times, restrictions on women, and the physical difficulty of most of the jobs, that most of the workers would be male. Since operative lodges worked independently of each other, it would seem reasonable that if women held some position in some of the lodges it could be unknown to other lodges. This would be especially true if Operative Masons, who were women, were rare and isolated cases.

While I hesitate to make any firm conclusion on if women ever served as Operative Freemasons, is clear that by the time the transition was made from Operative to Speculative Freemasonry the ban on women was established. From the earliest records of Speculative Freemasonry, it is clear that women were not allowed in Speculative Lodges of Freemasonry.

When we look back at history there are three periods of time that are important for this study: the Medieval Age, the Renaissance, and Age of Enlightenment.

Historians sometimes disagree on exactly when one age faded and another began, but we may look at, for general argument, that the Medieval Age ran from approximately 900

A.D. until 1300 A.D., the Renaissance from about 1300 A.D. until about 1700 A.D., and the Age of Enlightenment following that time.

Of course, these times are estimates and just as different societies can have different customs, attitudes, and traditions, so can traits from one period vary from place to place. One area may seem like a society from the Medieval Age while another well into the Renaissance.

By looking at the *Regius Manuscript* and noting that it is said to have been written about 1390 A.D., this places it at the beginning of the Renaissance period. It is in this manuscript where it is suggested that men and women could have worked together in Operative Lodges.

Let's look at this a bit.

The Renaissance is considered to be far more progressive, advanced in education, thought, and sciences than the Medieval Age. Certainly, the Renaissance was the golden age for Operative Freemasonry. It was during the Renaissance when so many of the magnificent European cathedrals and other beautiful structures were built by the old Operatives. But with all the advances that took place in the various societies during the Renaissance, there was one area that not only did not progress very far but it actually backtracked. This area was the role of women in society and their civil rights.

Even with the medieval culture being what it was, many argue that the role of women was even more limited during the Renaissance than during the Medieval Age.

During the Renaissance, women had no standing at all in society and few, if any, legal rights.

Operative Freemasonry was a profession that was dependent upon satisfied customers. It would seem logical that as society changed so did the face of Operative Freemasonry. Where during the Medieval Age it may have been impractical, in most cases, to have women as Operative Freemasons, it was possible. If the work was done properly, no one would have likely cared. But it seems that during the Renaissance, many *would have* cared if they saw a woman holding such a position.

The *Regius Manuscript* may have been reflective of Operative Freemasonry during the Medieval Age, and the absence of mention in later records and manuscripts of women in Masonry may be reflective of the change in attitude towards women during the Renaissance. But this is only an assumption. What is clear is that when Speculative Freemasonry came into being, there is good cause to view it as being modeled after the Royal Society of London.

The Royal Society was sometimes known as the "invisible college," due to its determination to do scientific research during periods of time when to do so was very much in disfavor. To be named a Fellow of the Royal Society was, and is, one of the highest honors one could or can achieve. The Royal Society was organized in the 1600s during the height of the Renaissance. While there is no clear prohibition on women being elected to membership or fellowship, it simply did not happen in those early days. Women had one place in society and men another.

Speculative Freemasonry's early ban on women simply followed the lead of the Royal Society and society in general. What is also very clear is that when Speculative Freemasonry was showcased to the world, it became very popular and quickly spread around the globe.

Soon after the creation of the Grand Lodge of England, Masonry spread to France. Like Masonry in England, Masonic lodges in France were for men only. But the French soon introduced a change in Masonic practice. The wives of Masons were brought to Masonic dinners and other events outside of the lodge. This was something that was not initially done in England.

What we must understand is that with the creation of the Grand Lodge of England, Masonry may have modeled itself on the Royal Society and the Renaissance attitude, but society was moving into the Age of Enlightenment. One of the key elements of the Age of Enlightenment was women's rights. France seems to have been slightly ahead of England in this social change.

Not very long after, France introduced an even more controversial creation. While Masonic lodges were reserved for men only, there was a desire to have something in which women could participate. Lodges of Adoption were created. Rituals were written that were clearly unconnected to Freemasonry yet had the same tone and recognition of the importance of initiation. Lodges of Adoption were not Masonic lodges, but they were the next best thing.

In his paper, *Women and Freemasonry*,[1] Dudley Wright presents us with an example of the ritual used by some of these Lodges of Adoption. The Lodges of Adoption became very popular in many areas of Europe except for England. As society moved further into the Age of Enlightenment, many women asked a very simple question, "Why can't I become a Freemason?" When no logical answer was given, female, and Co-Masonic lodges were created.

For the most part, Freemasonry arrived in America much as it was practiced in the United Kingdom. This would include the same position on women and Masonry as well as Lodges of Adoption. It would seem that Lodges of Adoption were viewed by British Masonry as cleverly disguised female Masonry.

Maybe it was indeed an objection to the Lodges of Adoption themselves or the fact that the French had created it, I'm not sure. But like in England, Lodges of Adoption were not popular in the United States. Then something happened in 1850 that changed everything.

Rob Morris, a Mississippi Mason of less than five years, created the rituals for what he called the Order of the Eastern Star in 1850. Morris may have learned of the Lodges of Adoption, or he may have simply wanted to create something for the female relatives of Masons. Regardless, Morris wrote a ritual that was of the same tone as the Lodges of Adoption, meaning: religious in nature, structured in degrees, and with initiations.

Following the Civil War, Morris turned over the Eastern Star to fellow Mason, Robert McCoy. McCoy revised the rituals, and the Eastern Star was not only a success but a major international success with chapters today in most areas of the world.

But the movement really didn't end there. Before long there were Masonic youth groups for boys such as DeMolay, youth groups for girls such as the Rainbow Girls and Job's Daughters, and other "side orders" for women with male family members belonging to various other Masonic bodies.

By the mid-1900s, Masonry truly became a family-oriented organization with various groups for any member of the family, all with Masonic themes or tones. Of course, the Eastern Star was not welcomed with open arms everywhere. To date, the United Grand Lodge of England does not allow its members to join the Eastern Star. It could be that the Eastern Star too closely resembles Co-Masonry for their taste. But bodies such as the Eastern Star as well as Lodges of Adoption only *resemble* Masonic lodges. The rituals of these "side orders" are clearly something other than Masonic.

In the early 1800s, Masonic lodges started appearing composed of both men and women as well as solely female Masonic lodges. Actual Masonic rituals were used in these bodies, and the clear desire was that they be viewed as Masonic lodges. Of course, these lodges were not recognized as regular, at least not initially, but they persisted.

In 1999, the United Grand Lodge of England made what many consider an astonishing announcement. They announced that two Grand Lodges composed of female Masons (The Order of Women Freemasons and The Honorable Fraternity of Ancient Freemasons) were, as far as they could determine, regular in nature, except that they were composed of women. While such a statement does not constitute fraternal relations nor is inter-visitation with these lodges allowed, it is still an amazing statement. The United Grand Lodge of England stated that these two females only Grand Lodges may be viewed *as regular*. That is an amazing statement. Of course, this statement did not include Co-Masonic lodges, nor did they lift their ban on their members belonging to the Eastern Star. But it is an amazing step.

As for male only lodges and Grand Lodges, they have been only a handful of cases where it has been reported that a woman was made a member of a Speculative Lodge of Freemasons. The earliest case reported is that of Elizabeth Aldworth. The date she is said to have been made a Mason is sometimes disputed, being either just before or just after 1717 in England, but that she was made a Mason does seem to be generally recognized.

The report is that Elizabeth was reading a book in her father's home in a small room next to the library when she fell asleep. At that time, it was common for Masonic lodges to meet in the homes of influential Masons. It seems that such a lodge meeting was held in her father's large library. The lodge then began an Entered Apprentice initiation. Elizabeth woke, and hearing voices in the room next to her, she went to investigate. Upon seeing the initiation taking place, she became curious and watched for a while. Upon being discovered by the lodge Tyler, she fainted. The lodge, being unsure of how to deal with the situation, decided that the best solution was to initiate her.

There are only a handful of other accounts where women, for one reason or another, have been said to have been initiated into a Speculative Lodge. Even if all of these accounts are completely correct, it is only a small number and only because of extenuating circumstances. For the most part, Speculative Freemasonry that is deemed to be recognized and regular has been kept male only. Why? I don't really know.

There are many articles and books written on the psychology of male fraternities and the suggested need for male bonding. Gentleman only clubs have existed for generations. The apparent need for men to gather on their own, away from women, has been suggested by some psychologists as a throwback to the very early days of man when the males would gather in hunting parties to bring home food. Whether this is true or not, instinct or not, there does seem to be a desire to keep male Masonry, male only. The exact reason this desire exists may be unknown, but it does seem to exist.

We live in a world today that is very different than in the 1500's, 1600's or 1700's. Women are not the property of their fathers or their husbands. They are not without citizenship or civil rights. As Speculative Freemasons we do not do hard, manual labor in our lodges. Our world is also very different than the 1800's or 1900's as well. As far as technology is concerned, we have made unimaginable technological advances. What we view as everyday tools of communication would be viewed as magic in the Medieval days.

But as human beings, I don't believe that we have advanced anywhere near the level that our technology has advanced. We still have the same fears, jealousies, personal dreams, and emotional frailties that were held by our medieval ancestors. I believe that we will always continue to use our mind to create amazing things, but that same mind can limit us through our emotional insecurities.

I've always heard that the male ego is a fragile thing. Are there legitimate reasons why women cannot take part in what we do in speculative lodges? Does the fragile male ego keep us separate, maybe out of concern that females will see our lodge meetings as shallow and nonsensical? Or is there no real answer and women are not allowed in Masonic lodges simply because *that is the way it has always been done*? I don't have an answer. But I do believe that time will provide the answer, no matter if we live to see that answer or not.

Notes:

1. Dudley Wright "Women and Freemasonry" *Masonic Enlightenment* (New Orleans, LA: Cornerstone Book Publishers, 2006) pp. 71-92.

Is Freemasonry Christian?

Recently, I was speaking with a Brother who told me of a paper that he had read in a Masonic publication suggesting that Freemasonry is a "Christian" organization. He said that he strongly disagreed with that position. Not having read the paper, I couldn't comment on what the author may have intended, but I found the subject interesting.

I always have been fascinated by word usage. With an understanding of how certain words are understood, we can communicate exactly what we mean, or, if we have enough skill, use certain words that provide multiple meanings. Politicians and salesmen are sometimes skilled in this practice when they say something that they know will be understood one way, only to actually mean something completely different.

When caught in a false, or unpopular statement, the clever trickster will cite these *other meanings* for what he said to get himself out of the trap. Some anti-Masons have also long been fond of selective understanding concerning pretty much anything written by Freemasons. To this day, Albert Pike is quoted by anti-Masons as "proof" that Freemasonry is a religion or unacceptable to Christians because of things offered in Pike's *Morals and Dogma* and other writings. In truth, Pike's word usage *is* sometimes difficult to understand and open to several different interpretations. Because of Pike's word selection, he provides anti-Masons with the perfect fodder for their attacks. I have no idea what Pike might have been thinking as he wrote, but I do acknowledge that it is possible that he knew exactly how his words might be misunderstood. If this is correct, it is possible that he used the words he chose for his personal amusement or refusal to be limited in what he was allowed to write.

The word "Christian" is another word that can be crystal clear or used in a way to lead readers in one direction while the author is going somewhere else. The anti-Masons provide a good example. We should not assume that the word "Christian" means the same thing to everyone.

One anti-Masonic group has a specific interpretation of the word "Christian" and offers it as their "proof" that Freemasonry is unsuitable for Christians. To them, a Christian is someone who has exactly the same beliefs and religious understandings as *they* hold. Period. If one believes *anything* differently from them, then regardless of what they profess, they are not accepted as a Christian.

In addition, some believe that a Christian should not associate with anyone who is not viewed as a Christian. Since Freemasonry is open to the worthy regardless of their faith, they cannot see a way that it could be acceptable to *their* concept of Christianity.

It is their understanding and use of the word "Christian" that defines their position. Even if their understanding of the word is contrary to everyone else, it is still *their* understanding of the word. For them, Freemasonry would be unsuitable.

But there are other thoughts about the word "Christian." The Roman Catholic Church claims to be the direct, original, and authentic Christian Church. It was certainly around prior to the Protestant Reformation of the 16th-century. The result of this reformation was the many new "Protestant" faiths that identified themselves as Christian but void of the alleged Catholic abuses and suggested deviations from the teachings of the Bible.

But was this reformation really the first one or, even, the most significant?

Around 300 AD, Constantine the Great pretty much overhauled the Christian Church, making it the Roman Catholic Church. Very few aspects of the church were left untouched. So, what was the Church before Constantine? That seems to be a matter of debate.

But what is not under debate is the name "Catholic Church." When spelled with a lower case "c," it means universal or all encompassing. I find that interesting.

Some believe that the original Christian Church or, Catholic Church, was far more esoteric in nature with many practices that Constantine felt compelled to replace. In fact, in some esoteric thought, the word "Christian" has the same meaning and understanding as "catholic." Christianity, in this context, is universal and all encompassing. It accepts all - like Freemasonry.

It does seem that some contradictory opinions exist concerning the meaning of the word "Christian." So, back to "Christian Freemasonry" — I don't know what the author of that paper had in his mind. Did he mean that Freemasonry should be open only to those who profess the Christian faith? Did he mean that Christianity is viewed by some as more esoteric than we realize and is far more welcoming and open to all? Or did he write with clever word usage that baffled more than informed? I don't know.

I do know, however, that we need to be careful about judging or accepting anything. I also know that Freemasonry is *not* designed or intended to limit itself to any one religious faith. To think otherwise is to misunderstand the nature of Freemasonry.

But some do try to write with a certain amount of dramatics that may be felt necessary to create an exciting paper but still offer them some protection should the paper be challenged. Conclusions that may seem obvious in a paper can be denied by the author as simply the reader misunderstanding the actual intent. Be careful of these types of writers.

Freemasonry is simply not a Christian only organization unless we use the word in a specific esoteric manner which should clearly be spelled out in a paper. Buyer, or reader beware.

Forgetting Your Lines

I'd like to write a few words that deal with what is really a fact of life for anyone who takes part in any Masonic degree. It is when things go wrong because of you, and you completely mess up your part of a degree. Now, we all know, or should know, that rehearsals are indispensable for all degree work. No one should accept, or be given, any office in lodge if they do not have the time or the ability to properly perform the work necessary for the office. But let's deal only with the conscientious officer who does spend the time necessary to learn his work only to fall victim to going completely blank during a degree. And let's be honest. This happens to everyone who performs ritual over any amount of time.

No matter how well you know the work, or how diligently you study and rehearse, there will be times when you completely draw a blank and have no idea what you are to say next. You may have been thrown off by someone sneezing, or some side conversation, or even seeing someone on the sidelines that you didn't expect to see in lodge. Anything can distract you and cause you to forget your lines.

How you handle yourself if and when you do draw a blank will be the difference between a good ritualist and someone only capable of memorizing a collection of words. The foundation of a good ritualist is knowing the work. You cannot get around the need to be proficient. But one of the dangers of memorizing the work for a degree, and doing well in a degree, is the degree that follows.

Let me explain.

If you ask someone what they had for dinner on Wednesday two weeks ago, most people will not be able to tell you. We don't keep information like that readily available in our memory because it's not useful or necessary. We remember things that we believe are necessary to remember.

In school, we all studied for tests on a variety of subjects. Many times, we had little interest in a particular subject, but we needed to remember certain things to pass a test to get out of the class. We remembered what we needed to remember for the test. When we graduated or were no longer in that class, we often forgot most all that we had learned for any of the tests for that subject. It was no longer necessary to keep that information in our memory. If we are not careful, the same thing can happen with ritual work.

If we memorize the ritual, learn it well, and then do well in our performance, it is possible that we will assume that we permanently know this work. If we then fail to review it enough for the next degree, we could end up having a poor degree with many errors.

So, when the inevitable does happen (no matter if due to not rehearsing enough or some unforeseen event) and you do draw a blank and forget what you are to say next, how you handle it will determine your skill as a ritualist. The absolute most important thing is to stay calm. Remember, the candidate not only has no idea what you will say next, but he has no idea that any mistake was made – unless it is made clear to him. If you fall apart, stumble around, or lose it completely, he will certainly know that something is wrong, and the degree could be ruined for him.

Take a beat. Take a moment to stop, calm yourself and gather your wits. Many times, what you forgot will come right back to you, and you can move on with no real disturbance to the degree. How you act will determine in a large part how well what you say is received by the candidate.

There is no getting around the fact that we need to learn the work. There is also no getting around the fact that no matter how well we know the ritual, there will be times when our memory fails us. When this happens, we need to stop, collect ourselves and remain calm. Do not focus on the fact that something was forgotten. That will only upset you more and compound the problem. Clear your mind and relax.

If that does not bring the next lines back to you, then calmly look to someone for help. A prompter experienced in the work should be in every lodge. He should be the one responsible for giving lines when needed (not everyone on the sidelines yelling out corrections). Look to him and once the next lines are given, move on.

Staying relaxed and calm is the best way to help with your memory and keep the atmosphere of the degree beneficial to the candidate.

Weapons in Lodge

I wanted to write something today on a subject that may be a bit of a hot button topic with some or, maybe, a number of Masons. It's the subject of weapons in lodges.

As with so much today in Masonry, and really the world, we seem to be in a time of great division. You will see individuals on one side of some question who are very passionate in their opinion regarding...well, anything. You will then see others who are equally enthusiastic about a completely opposite position. Both are fixed, unchanging and determined. Hostile outbursts between the groups are common.

In reading several on-line debates recently on Masonic forums concerning guns in lodge, I've come to see the strong opinions many have on the subject. Let's look at this situation.

The lodge I joined in the mid 1970's happened to have a good number of police officers as members. The WM was a lieutenant in the New Orleans Police Department. Virtually all of the line officers were members of one of the area law enforcement agencies. I remember something that was done almost as a ritual before lodge. Each one of the police officers, and I mean in uniform or not, would remove his gun from its holster, empty the weapon, put the shells in his pocket (so that the gun would not go off when it was not in his control), and then turn the gun over to the tiler. The tiler would then place it in a secure box in his care. The tiler would oversee all guns until the conclusion of the lodge meeting.

I once asked them why they did this. I was reminded of our ritual. It states that nothing offensive nor defensive would be brought into the lodge. Our third degree was also often cited. And I also received confused and astonished stares at my question. I was told rather loudly, "It's a *lodge!* You don't bring a *gun* into a lodge!" No matter what anyone believes is proper or improper today, this *was* the practice at that time in all the lodges that I visited, and it was the policy for as long as anyone could remember. But that was then, and this is now.

Today, it is common to see Masons who are in law enforcement, and many who are not, with weapons openly displayed in tiled lodges and even during degrees. I have on several occasions asked brothers openly wearing weapons during degrees to remove their weapon out of respect for the ceremony. I was met with angry responses. Actually, the ones *not* in law enforcement seemed to give the more hostile responses. I was told that they have permits to carry their guns and that this is their right. I was also told that they do not trust *anyone* in the lodge with their weapon, loaded or not.

Let's try to look at the differing opinions.

Those who carry weapons in lodge often cite their concern for personal safety. The idea is that they feel that carrying a weapon increases their odds should they encounter someone with a desire to do them harm.

On one on-line forum I saw the following post, and I will give you exactly what he wrote. The Brother said,

> *"I am a law enforcement officer and have been for many years. When I became a Mason some members of my lodge told me I couldn't come to lodge with my weapon. I told them I wouldn't come to lodge if I couldn't be armed. There are evil men in the world, and I am charged to protect. Additionally, I've had to arrest members of our fraternity so I could easily run into something inside the lodge as well as out."*

OK, let's think about what that brother wrote for a minute. There are a few things that I believe we should look at a bit closer. The brother said that he is "charged to protect." I would assume that this means all around him as well as himself. But are his obligations to protect greater, or different, than those police officers who were members of my Mother lodge in the 1970's? Not even one of them carried a loaded weapon in a tiled lodge. If the civic obligations are the same, then could something else have changed? There are two other things that he wrote that caught my attention. He said that he would not come to lodge if he were not allowed to bring his weapon. This makes me think that he has some serious concern for his safety, or that going to lodge is not really that important to him.

But what is possibly even more telling is what he wrote next. He said, "I've had to arrest members of our fraternity so I could easily run into something *inside* the lodge as well as out." What does he mean by that statement? Does he mean that it is possible that someone he once arrested might have gotten off, be a member of a lodge near him, and might shoot him in his lodge? Or could he mean that if *some* Masons can commit crimes, then others can as well, so he has to be ready in case anyone attacks him, or someone else, in lodge?

This brother is either serious or not. He is either correct in his evaluation of Freemasons or he is not. If he is serious and if he is correct in his evaluation, then this is a horrible contradiction of the professed nature of Freemasonry. We profess to be a moral organization. But what have we allowed ourselves to become? We say to the world that our role is to take good men and make them better. Exactly what do we mean by "better?"

If members seriously and legitimately feel that those who sit in lodge with them might take their life, and their concern is great enough that they need to arm themselves, then maybe we should admit that we have horribly failed in our declared mission. Maybe we should close our doors right now. But is his reason for carrying a weapon in lodge the same as others who also believe that they should be armed in lodge? Maybe not.

Other Masons who I have spoken to about guns in lodges as well as comments made on various forums give other reasons for wishing to be armed while in lodge. It is not that these brothers are so worried about members of *the lodge* attacking them as much as criminals *outside* of the lodge. Some fear walking from their lodge to their car. Others say that they fear a terrorist or crazed anti-Mason breaking into the lodge and killing the members inside. Let's look at these situations.

Crime does exist. People are shot and killed in large cities and small towns all over the world. Mass shootings have taken place in locations where we never believed could see such horror. It is reasonable for people to have concerns about their safety and take precautions to protect themselves. But what I just said is subjective. Exactly what is reasonable and what is unreasonable? How can I know the level of another person's fear for his safety?

In my younger years, I studied martial arts. One of the first things that I was taught was street safety. I was taught to always be aware of my soundings. If you are unaware of what is going on around you, someone can basically walk right up to you and do whatever they want. The second thing was that no matter how big and bad you are, there is *always* someone bigger and badder. Our very best weapon is our brain.

When someone carries a gun, it can give them an advantage in certain situations (if they know how to use it) but it will not make them invincible. I was taught that the most important thing someone can do on the street is to be aware of all around him. If he sees something that feels bad or looks wrong, then he should get away from it. Walk, run, do whatever it takes, but get away. Only a fool knowingly walks into a bad situation.

If someone is legally entitled to carry a gun, then the ONLY time that he should pull it, is if there is absolutely nothing else that he can do, if he fears for his life, and if he is ready to kill the one threatening him. Anything else can only get him in much more trouble. Another thing that I was taught (and it should really be a no brainer), is that when out at night (and there is a concern for safety), we should walk in a group. Criminals like easy targets. Someone out by himself is a far more attractive target than a group of men. But this is discussing events that could happen when someone leaves or goes to a lodge. It is not dealing with anything inside of the lodge. So, if someone fears walking to his car from the lodge, then why would he need to carry a weapon inside a tiled lodge? Well, I've also heard some answers to that question.

I've heard some say that a concern for them is that someone could come into the lodge hall, shoot everyone downstairs, and then come up and shoot everyone in the lodge itself. A gun is felt to be needed in the lodge in the event someone comes into the lodge with the intent of killing members. While I find this only a remote possibility in any location, I can't say that it is impossible.

We have all read of someone going into schools, churches, movie theaters, and a good number of other places and just opening fire on whoever was around. It is random killings by a sick person. We have also heard of someone going into a business or other such place with the intent of shooting one person and then shooting others just because they happened to be there. These things have happened. People are losing control and doing all sorts of things. In fact, is it not impossible to think that the guy with the gun in lodge might flip out, pull his gun, and start shooting at everyone in lodge himself? Could this be the reason the police officer on the on-line forum wanted to be armed in lodge? Could he be concerned by some of the ones in lodge who also have weapons and wants his weapon in case any of them starts shooting? It's getting crazy.

In my opinion, if someone is concerned about trouble *outside* of the lodge, then he should walk to his car in a group, or he should retrieve his weapon from the tiler after the lodge meeting is over, and then go to his car. If someone is worried about their safety *inside* of the lodge from outside attack, then they can lock the outside doors once the lodge starts, arm their tiler, or hire private armed security for the lodge. If someone is seriously worried about their safety from members *inside* of their lodge, then I suggest they find another lodge. That lodge is light years from being a true Masonic lodge.

I see no valid reason to carry a loaded weapon in a tiled lodge other than ... well, this is just want the individual wants to do. I find it extraordinarily inappropriate to openly display a gun in a tiled lodge due to the religious, solemn, and educational nature of a lodge. If someone is legally entitled to carry a weapon and he has a concern for his safety, then if he *must* carry a gun, *conceal it*. No one has to know about it. Have enough respect for the ceremony not to have it in everyone's face.

I've seen Masons on a degree team carrying large military handguns strapped to their hips in full display during degrees. Just because these Masons are ignorant of the nature and meaning of Masonic initiation does not mean that the nature and meanings do not exist. I believe that the entire subject of weapons in lodge and the great division in the members as to if it is proper or improper mirrors the division in Masonry on many subjects.

We do see some lodges striving to be centers of Masonic education and others desiring little more than social club status. How a lodge operates and conducts itself is reflective of how it will deal with the question of weapons in lodge.

For whatever it is worth, my opinion is that there is no place for weapons in a tiled lodge. Our lodges are sacred places for spiritual and moral growth. I believe that to carry a weapon into a lodge is to disgrace it. If one has a sincere concern about his safety, then lock the doors of the lodge. Hire armed security. Arm the tiler. Walk to and from your car in groups. Carry your weapon to and from the lodge, leaving it with the tiler while in lodge. Or, if your safety concern is great enough and serious enough — stay home. Your life is worth more than a lodge meeting.

Ultimately, however, I realize that most will do whatever they wish and are allowed to do.

Notes:

1. A quote attributed to Isaac Disraeli.

What's the Deal with the Scottish Rite?

Recently I have had a few brothers send me e-mails, and actually, a few have spoken to me in person, about issues they have with certain aspects of the Scottish Rite. Their complaint, as best as they have told me, is that they are disappointed that the Scottish Rite does not act democratic, and they always add, "as it is supposed to act." Well, this comes from a basic misunderstanding of the Scottish Rite. Let's start at the beginning. And, for this discussion, we will deal only with the Supreme Council, Southern Jurisdiction, USA.

The Southern Jurisdiction has 33 Active Members. These are the members who can speak and vote in a supreme council session. They have received the 33rd degree and hold the office of Sovereign Grand Inspector General. They are known, for short, as an SGIG. Each SGIG normally has jurisdiction over an Orient, which is normally a state. They are responsible for all aspects of the Scottish Rite within their jurisdiction. All decisions made in an Orient are made by the SGIG.

Most of the time, but this is not set in stone, an SGIG will first serve as a Deputy of the Supreme Council. When an SGIG retires, dies, or for whatever reason leaves office, the Supreme Council will appoint someone to head the Scottish Rite in that state. Normally, someone who has received the 33rd degree and is an honorary Sovereign Grand Inspector General, more commonly known as a *White Cap*, will be appointed as a Deputy. They will oversee the Scottish Rite in that jurisdiction. At some point, they may be elected by the Supreme Council as an SGIG. An SGIG normally serves until the age of 80.

It is the relationship between the members of the Scottish Rite and the Active Members of the Supreme Council that confuses most Scottish Rite Masons. Every year, Scottish Rite Valleys elect new officers for the various bodies. The Valleys may elect or appoint various members to serve on boards, degree teams, and fill any office or position that may be necessary. What must be understood is that while most of the time these elections and appointments seem final and made by the Valley, they are in fact, and technically, only recommendations made by the Valley to the SGIG. It is the SGIG who makes the actual appointments — even if it is done passively by not overruling the Valley. It is the SGIG who approves, or in some cases, does not approve the actions of a Valley. Most of the time elections and appointments are accepted as almost routine, or automatic, but it must be understood that within an Orient or state, it is the SGIG, or Deputy, who has the final say in everything. He is the only voice or vote for the Scottish Rite in a particular Orient. At any time, an SGIG can overrule any action, election, or appointment of a Valley. I believe that this misunderstanding of the nature of the Scottish Rite comes from a belief that

Valley elections or appointments carry the same weight as the vote or decision made by lodges in a Grand Lodge session. This is simply not correct.

As far as the Scottish Rite is concerned, the entire authority of the Grand Lodge rests within an SGIG. The democratic nature of the Scottish Rite takes place in the Supreme Council session where the SGIG's vote is counted as one of 33 votes.

When the SGIGs gather in the Supreme Council, then each has a single vote, and it is here that the democratic process takes place. With this understanding, we can see the scope of the responsibility and authority of an SGIG. It is within their authority to approve or disapprove anything at all within their Orient. In most cases, decisions made by a Valley are approved by the SGIG as a matter of routine. They normally make sure that those in Valley leadership are ones that they can trust and whose opinion is of value to them. From a practical sense, it would be an almost impossible job, especially in large Orients, for an SGIG to make every possible decision for every Valley. In most cases, an SGIG would only step in if he felt there was a serious need to do so.

Obviously, because of the tremendous responsibility placed upon an SGIG, the Supreme Council tries to select and elect only those of outstanding ability. When good selections are made an Orient can prosper and grow. If a poor selection is made, then damage to the Orient can be almost assured. If an SGIG is lacking in ability, then we can see a downward slide for the whole of the Scottish Rite within an Orient. Ultimately, the success or failure of the Scottish Rite within an Orient can be traced to the SGIG or Deputy. The decisions that they make, the appointments & elections that they approve, and the course that they set for their Orient will all play a part in the success or failure of the Scottish Rite in their jurisdiction.

With such a heavy responsibility placed upon them, it is understandable that an SGIG may from time to time overrule a Valley in a decision that they make or seem to change some particular policy or person to one that they believe will best serve the Scottish Rite. They will do this normally *not* because of any desire to show their power but because they realize that if the Scottish Rite fails, slides downward, or is anything but the best that it can be, then it is ultimately *his* failure. Such a failure will be recognized by the Supreme Council and all who understand the workings of the Scottish Rite.

So, when we look at the democratic nature of the Scottish Rite, we have to understand how the system works and operates. We need to understand the chain of authority and responsibilities placed upon the various individuals in authority. The officers of the Valley need to perform their duties to the best of their abilities, but it needs to be understood that all serve at the will and pleasure of the SGIG.

Since it is the SGIG who is ultimately responsible for the success or failure of all valleys within his jurisdiction, then he wants to be sure that he has the best people in office who can best serve the Scottish Rite.

The First Three of the Thirty-Three Degrees of the Ancient and Accepted Scottish Rite

It's often said that Freemasonry is a beautiful system of morality, veiled in allegory and illustrated by symbols. We read in Masonic books and hear in Masonic lectures that the primary goal of Freemasonry is to take good men and make them better. But how do we do that? We teach them. We educate our members using our ancient teaching methods to improve ourselves, chip away at imperfections, and make us better human beings, better members of society, and consequently happier.

Albert Mackey is quoted as writing, "The ultimate success of Masonry depends on the intelligence of her disciples." I find that a very interesting quote as he seems to qualify the actual success of Freemasonry as well as the intelligence of its members. Mackey is not telling us that Masonry *is* successful because of the intelligence of its members. He is telling us that Masonry *will be* successful *if* it has intelligent members. Our lodges will have intelligent members if the lodges provide Masonic education. Our members will be educated and intelligent in Masonry if they take advantage of the education that is offered. If our members do not take advantage of the educational opportunities, or if the lodges provide nothing other than a hot meal and a reading of the minutes, then the "ultimate success" that brother Mackey spoke of will not take place.

One area of Masonic education that I would like to explore today has to do with the nature of Masonic rites. I find today that many in the United States confuse or have but limited understanding of the actual differences between a Masonic rite and an appendant body. They are different animals.

In the US, many, to most, consider an appendant body as pretty much anything other than a craft lodge. Repeatedly I read in US Masonic publications and hear in lectures that the York Rite and the Scottish Rite are *appendant bodies*. When questioned as to why these two rites are considered appendant, I'm normally either given a blank stare or told that anything other than a craft lodge is defined as an appendant body.

Of course, organizations such as the Shrine, the Grotto, the Eastern Star, and many other like organizations are also considered appendant bodies. With these organizations, I completely agree with how they are identified.

But let me explain why I do not consider the York Rite and the Scottish Rite as appendant bodies. Both the York Rite and the Scottish Rite are Masonic rites, or systems of Freemasonry. A rite, or system of Freemasonry, is a collection of unique rituals beginning in the entered apprentice degree and concluding in whatever is their final degree.

The Scottish Rite and the York Rite are both considered as *Masonic rites* because they both began in the entered apprentice degree. The shrine, grotto, Eastern Star, and other like bodies do not begin their first actual degree or ceremony in the entered apprentice degree.

As a prerequisite, many of these organizations require membership in a craft lodge, meaning having obtained the degree of Master Mason. And here is the source of a long-held confusion.

Let me explain.

A Masonic ritual is the script that is used to confer degrees, open lodges, and is the words of our catechism. While a Masonic craft ritual is normally viewed as one that will contain the Hiramic Legend, the actual words and actions of the ritual, or script, can change quite a bit depending on who is the author, or editor of that ritual. While the three craft degrees are similar to each other and follow a logical storyline, they can be quite different than other rituals of the same degrees. These differences can be looked at as the different *Rites of Freemasonry.* You can think of it as different ways of telling the same story.

When Speculative Freemasonry was taken from England to France in its very early days, a language problem existed. It was necessary to translate the early English rituals into French if there was going to be any hope of successfully spreading Freemasonry in France. It would seem that when this translation was done, some consideration for the French culture was given. When we compare early English rituals to early French rituals, it is very easy to see that the French rituals are more theatrical in nature. The French rituals also spent more time on symbolism than do the English rituals. I believe this has much to do with the two cultures and the differences in the rituals were reflections of the differences in those two cultures. We can trace quite several different rituals (or, rites) existing in the world today from both the early English and the early French rituals, but for the point of this study we will confine ourselves to the rituals that exist in the United States today.

If we look at Freemasonry that existed in what would become the United States of America just after the American Revolution, we can see some interesting developments. Most all of Freemasonry that existed in what would become the United States came from either England, Ireland, or Scotland. While variations in these rituals existed, they would all seem to have come from the same basic source.

The Freemasons in the young United States began reorganizing Freemasonry in their new country to suit their likes. Some consideration was given to having one Grand Lodge for the entire country. But it seems that the final plan was to mirror the example of the organization of the new government — meaning more consideration for the states. With that, it was felt that one Grand Lodge per state was their best choice. In the years that followed, Freemasonry in the United States began refining its nature and defining what it wanted out of each Grand Lodge. The general consensus was that each Grand Lodge should be as near as possible a copy of the other. Each would be sovereign and independent, yet very similar in the craft lodge experience to the other Grand Lodges.

There was a desire for there to be one Grand Lodge per state, one language per Grand Lodge (and that would be English) and one ritual for each Grand Lodge. When we try to understand *why* they wanted the early Grand Lodges to set up this way, we cannot look to any of the ancient charges for answers. The only answer that is logical for why they wanted the US Grand Lodges so like each other is because ... that's what they wanted. Period.

So, with this one Grand Lodge, one language, and one ritual concept, the various Grand Lodges began to organize and refine themselves. Representatives of the various Grand Lodges would meet regularly to discuss the progress of Masonry in the US. But there was a problem for them in one area, and that area was South Carolina. To understand the situation in South Carolina, we will need to take a quick look at England.

Without getting into a lengthy history of Freemasonry in England, two groups having different Masonic philosophies developed in England prior to 1800. One styled themselves as the Ancients and the other as the Moderns. These two Grand Lodges in England were, to say the least, unfriendly towards each other. But they did end up settling their differences and in 1813 merged into what we have today as the United Grand Lodge of England.

In South Carolina, just prior to 1800 there were also two Grand Lodges in that state, each representing one of the two styles of Freemasonry in England. Both were considered perfectly regular. But the problem remained that the collective desire of the US Grand Lodges was that there be one Grand Lodge per state.

Pressure began being placed on South Carolina for these two Grand Lodges to merge. The problem was that they didn't like each other and found the others' Masonic philosophy wholly unacceptable. They simply did not want to merge.

In 1801, a new development and a new problem came with the creation of a third Masonic body in South Carolina. This body did not trace itself back to the English style of Freemasonry, but to the French style.

Throughout the Caribbean islands, a French style of Masonry called the Order of the Royal Secret, but more commonly known as the Rite of Perfection had gained significant popularity. This was a 25-degree system of French style Masonry that was very unique and quite different than the English style of Freemasonry.

The problem was that it was very poorly organized and lacked any central leadership. A handful of Masons who had reached the highest degree in this French system met in Charleston, South Carolina to discuss the problems with this system. Their solution was to create a new system with a better organization. The result of this new creation is what we have today as the 33-degree *Ancient and Accepted Scottish Rite*.

Keep in mind, this new 33-degree French style system, like the old 25 degree system, was a complete system that included its own unique craft degrees. The two oldest known rituals of the old 25-degree system in the US are the *Francken Manuscript* and the *Bonseigneur Rituals*. We'll talk a little more about them in a minute.

So, when this new 33-degree system was created in Charleston, its birth certificate claims to begin in the Entered Apprentice degree.[1] But there was a clear problem. South Carolina was already under considerable pressure because they had two grand bodies controlling craft degrees. The US Grand Lodge community wanted these two bodies to merge so that there would be one. The idea that a *third body* would be allowed, which also controlled the craft degrees, was unthinkable.

While most all early records of the Charleston Supreme Council (known today as the Southern Jurisdiction) do not exist, we can assume that there was strong objection to this new body controlling craft degrees. If the young Charleston Council ever did attempt to work in the craft degrees of the Scottish Rite, it would certainly have been short-lived. But we have no information one way or the other. All that we know from the records that exist is that at some point the Supreme Council clearly confined its degrees from the 4th to the 33rd.

Such was not the case, however, with the second, third and fourth supreme councils to be created. Each of these *did* work in the complete 33 degrees of the Ancient and Accepted Scottish Rite, beginning in their own unique craft lodge ritual. The second and third supreme councils were located in the Caribbean islands and the fourth was the Supreme Council of France.

Finally, the two Grand Lodges in South Carolina did merge into one and the Charleston Supreme Council *did not* work in the craft degrees, so all was well in the US world of Freemasonry — at least for a time. New Orleans was founded by the French in 1718. The first documented evidence of a

Masonic lodge in New Orleans was in 1752. The area was French in language and nature. Likewise, so was the Freemasonry.

The Grand Lodge of Louisiana was created in 1812 by five French-speaking lodges. The Grand Lodge itself was French-speaking and organized much like many of the European Grand Lodges. Like so much of the early history of the Scottish Rite, great holes exist in the history of early Louisiana Masonry. Many aspects of early Masonry in Louisiana remain a mystery to this day. For example, in which ritual, or rituals, did these early five lodges work? Or even, in which ritual did the Grand Lodge itself originally work? We simply cannot answer with any certainty.

This brings us back to what was mentioned earlier about the *Francken Manuscript* and the *Bonseigneur Rituals*. These two documents are collections of rituals of the old Order of the Royal Secret — the 25-degree system from which the rituals of the 33 degree Ancient and Accepted Scottish Rite built upon. The two collections date from around the same time but clear differences exist in them.

I won't go into any technical differences in the rituals themselves, but I will mention two very clear and obvious differences. For one, the *Francken Manuscript* is written in English and the *Bonseigneur Rituals* in French. The second clear difference is that the *Francken Manuscript* begins with the fourth degree and the *Bonseigneur Rituals* with the first degree — the Entered Apprentice degree.

It would seem that the *Francken Manuscript* was written in English and began in the fourth degree out of awareness of the preference of the U.S. Masons. The *Bonseigneur Rituals* were, however, worked in an area that was not bound to these customs. They were free to work in French and the complete system.

While we cannot be certain as to the actual ritual of the early Louisiana lodges or the Grand Lodge itself, we can make certain reasonable assumptions. The rituals would have to have been valid and accepted rituals to the Masons of the area, they would have had to have been available, and they would have to have been in the French language. The *Bonseigneur Rituals* fit the bill in each of these cases.

While it is impossible to say with certainty, it is very possible that this ritual, or one very similar to it, was the Louisiana Masonic ritual at the time of the creation of the Grand Lodge of Louisiana. While there are many holes in our understanding of early Louisiana Masonry, there are bits and pieces of information that can help us with this puzzle.

We know from discovered records[2] that *le Bennifiance Lodge #1* was created in New Orleans in 1807. It was created by Sovereign Grand Inspectors General under the jurisdiction of the 1804 Supreme Council of Kingston, Jamaica.[2] This supreme council was the third council to be created and was in full relations with the Charleston Supreme Council.[3] In 1809, these same SGIG's created a Lodge of Perfection in New Orleans and then in 1811, a Grand Consistory. This 1811 Grand Consistory exists today as the Valley of New Orleans. This 1807 New Orleans lodge was a craft lodge of the Ancient and Accepted Scottish Rite, and it is the first such lodge that we can reasonably verify. But while this lodge existed at the time of the creation of the Grand Lodge, it was not one of the five lodges to create the Grand Lodge of Louisiana. The records are silent as to why they did not participate. The lodge did, however, merge with the oldest of the five lodges that created the Grand Lodge, Perfect Union # 1, not long after the creation of the Grand Lodge.

Another bit of evidence that we can point to is the reaction to New Orleans Masonry by those Masons who came into New Orleans from other parts of the US. The 1803 Louisiana Purchase brought an influx of American merchants and travelers to New Orleans, many of whom were Freemasons. But, the Masonry they found in New Orleans was at first perplexing and then frustrating.

By the early 1800's, Freemasonry in the U.S. was settling into the concept of one Grand Lodge, one language (English), and one ritual. That one ritual was hammered out and became the Preston/Webb ritual which is the foundation of most all U.S. craft rituals. But this was not the case in New Orleans.

In New Orleans, the traveling Masons not only found lodges working in different languages but also different rituals. It was, to say the least, confusing for them. The English-speaking American Masons traveling to New Orleans wanted their Masonic experience in New Orleans to be the same as their experience in any other American city. For the New Orleans lodges, and even Grand Lodge, they saw the demands of the English-speaking American Masons to be at the least rude and bordering on unMasonic. It was an impasse.

The Masonry that was being practiced in New Orleans was the same as had always been practiced. In addition, it was the same Masonry that was being practiced in Europe. The friction between the two groups turned into open hostility and the Grand Lodge's position of allowing the lodges to work whatever ritual they chose was under strong attack.

By the early 1830s, the Grand Lodge realized it needed to do something regarding the rituals worked by the New Orleans area lodges. The Grand Lodge needed to take charge. The solution of the Grand Lodge was to create a governing body within the Grand Lodge for the supervision of the ritual worked by the lodges. They named the new body, "The Chamber of Rites."

The Chamber of Rites was composed of three committees, or chambers, one for each of the Rites that were approved to be worked in the lodges. Individuals proven to be proficient in the York Rite, Scottish Rite, and French or Modern Rite rituals were placed in their respective chambers to supervise the rituals of the lodges. The Grand Lodge saw this as a responsible solution to the problem and was satisfied. The English-speaking American Masons, however, were very *dissatisfied.* They saw this Chamber of Rites as making matters only worse. They were very clear in what they wanted, and that was *one* Grand Lodge, *one* language (English), and *one* ritual. They wanted the Scottish Rite and French Rite rituals purged from the Grand Lodge of Louisiana. The situation became so hostile that the Grand Lodge became fractured and split into groups.

The mid-1840s saw a second Grand Lodge created in New Orleans along the lines of the wants and desires of the

English-speaking American Masons. The events that followed are extremely complex and lengthy. For this paper, it is enough to say that extremely unfortunate times were faced by Louisiana Freemasonry. For the next 40 to 50 years (and in some cases, longer), extremely bitter feelings were felt on all sides of the issue.

The French Rite ritual was either driven out or merged in with aspects of the Scottish Rite. All non-English and non-York Rite craft rituals were eventually confined to one district created in the New Orleans area — the 16th Masonic district.

Today, the 16th Masonic district of the Grand Lodge of Louisiana is composed of 10 lodges working in the Ancient and Accepted Scottish Rite craft rituals. Certainly, the Grand Lodge of Louisiana has the largest number of craft lodges working in the Scottish Rite ritual of the US Grand Lodges, but it is not alone. The Grand Lodges of New York, California, and Hawaii also have verified Scottish Rite ritual craft lodges. Outside of the United States, the Scottish Rite craft lodge ritual is one of the most popular rituals for well recognized Grand Lodges in Central America, South America, and Europe.

So, why is the Scottish Rite craft ritual so rare, and in some cases, outlawed by some US Grand Lodges? The ritual is profoundly rich and symbolic. It does nothing but add beauty and deep meaning to our teachings. I believe that in many cases, the real answer has been forgotten or twisted with time. I believe that one answer is "just because." Another answer is long held disapproval for reasons long forgotten. Yet another answer is that some consider the Scottish Rite craft ritual to be irregular. But the common Masonic practice is to find *bodies* either regular or irregular, not rituals. But, in the end, the heart of the problem is far simpler. I believe that in the very early days of our country, a decision was made to do something. It was a decision that we should all be the same. Everything and everyone who was the same, was good. Everything and everyone who was different, was bad. It's as simple as that. Of course, the problem is that we are *not* all the same.

To go back to Bro. Mackey's comment quoted at the beginning of this paper. It may seem that our intelligence as well as our success will be determined by how much we know. In the case of the first three degrees of the Ancient and Accepted Scottish Rite, it may seem that we need to know more. It's one thing to prefer one flavor of ice cream over another. It is quite another thing to perpetuate falsehoods of a flavor you have never even tried.

Notes:

1. See: Ray Baker Harris, James D. Carter *History of the Supreme Council, 33° Southern Jurisdiction, USA (1801-1861)* Washington, D.C.: The Supreme Council, 33° 1964) 319-325.
2. *Sharp Documents* located in the Archives of the Supreme Council Northern Masonic Jurisdiction USA.
3. R.F. Gould, W.J. Hughan, A.F.A. Woodword, D.M. Lyon, J.H. Drummond, E.T. Carson, T.S. Parvin - Editors, *A Library of Freemasonry, Vol. V* (Philadelphia: The John C. Yorston Publishing Co., 1923), 298-299.

The Sick Lodge

I believe that one of the biggest frustrations that individual Masons have with their lodge has to do with the direction that the lodge is going. It seems that the question of right or wrong, as far as the direction of a lodge, is very subjective. What's right for one lodge may be completely wrong for another. I think that the correct direction for a lodge is the direction desired by most of the members.

It is not necessary that all lodges do as you like. In fact, it's not possible. Because individuals have different likes and dislikes, you're going to find different paths taken by different lodges.

Of course, there is a new (or really, revival) wave in Masonry taking place. The deeper aspects of Masonic philosophy, history, and ritual are desired to be taught in the lodges by more members than in the recent past. But there are also many lodges which are more or less social or charity clubs. The members gather for an evening of conversation, maybe over a meal, and then some talk to plan a worthy charitable or social project. There is nothing in the world wrong with this type of lodge, unless the members want something more. There is also nothing in the world wrong with the lodge that teaches Masonic philosophy. This would be a lodge where at any meeting you may find some lecture on any one of the many deeper aspects of Freemasonry.

The problems come when you are in one type of lodge and expect something else from your lodge experience. Each of these problems would not necessarily be a problem of the lodge, but a problem for you as an individual.

If you are not satisfied, or happy, with what goes on in your lodge, yet the lodge is functioning well, has good attendance and all signs of success then how can anyone say that the lodge is doing something wrong? There is a big difference between a lodge that is floundering and a lodge that simply operates differently than someone may desire.

If you are not satisfied with the direction your lodge is going, then take a close look at it. If it is clear that the lodge is operating successfully, has no problems, and all of the members are happy, then the problem is you. Trying to change such a lodge to suit your own desires is not only unfair but rarely possible. Even if you were able to change such a lodge to make you personally happy, it would likely result in the majority of the members becoming unhappy and the future success of the lodge could be in question.

We need to realistically look at a situation, without emotion, and try to determine the best course of action for us as individuals and the lodge. There is no shame or harm in realizing that a successful lodge is going in a direction not desired by you. There is no shame in finding a new lodge.

Charges that you are being unfair, disloyal, or ungrateful to your lodge because you are leaving to seek something more in line with your view of Masonry are unfounded and should be disregarded. Everyone has the right to have their own desired Masonic experience.

If, however, your lodge is in trouble then you should do all that you can do to try and help your lodge. When someone puts out their hand and asks you for help, whenever possible, you should help them. But you should note what I just said, as well noting the qualifying phrase in our obligations. The qualifying phrase is, "if possible."

Let me try to explain.

I remember long ago as a boy hearing loud, angry yelling outside my house. I went outside and saw a neighbor doing something very strange. He was staggering down the middle of the street with his head back and arms outstretched yelling like a wild man. As a child, it shook me. My mother came out, grabbed me, and pulled me back into the house. She told me to stay inside and locked the door. She said that the neighbor was "ill."

Years later she told me more about that story. The neighbor was an alcoholic. His wife had done everything that could be done to try and help him. He would listen to no one.

Finally, after going to therapy, fighting with him, threatening him, and doing everything possible, the therapist had a stern conversation with the wife. He told her that there was nothing more that she could do to reach her husband. He said that unless *he* decided to change, he was not going to do so. He said that unless *he* understood that there was a problem, he was going to continue to drink himself to death. He said that there was nothing that she could do to force him to change or stop drinking. He told the wife that there was only one thing that she could do if she cared about him. She agreed to do it.

She took all the money out of the checking account, went to the grocery, stocked the refrigerator, the freezer, and the cabinets with food, made sure there was not a drop of liquor in the house, and she left him. The therapist said that it was necessary for him to reach rock bottom in order to help him.

What I saw coming down the street as a boy was the husband reaching rock bottom. The wife could no longer reason with him. She was blamed for all his troubles by leaving him. He had broken into the house of another neighbor, stole, and drank all his liquor, and was yelling at his wife and the world in the middle of the street.

What has this to do with a lodge that is in trouble? Well, we all have free will. Many times, we see, believe, and think whatever we want. If a lodge is in trouble, and by that I mean, low attendance, trouble filling chairs, in need of calling other lodges for degree work, and all the problems that go along with disinterest in a lodge, then the lodge may or may not recognize that they are in serious trouble.

If a lodge does not recognize that they are in trouble or refuses to do what is needed to bring the lodge back to health, then anyone who tries to help them may be seen as a trouble-maker. *They* may be seen as the problem. Whatever they say or suggest being done will be seen as the problem. The lodge would be in denial of their real problem and what is needed to fix it. They cannot be reached. If someone pushes them to make this or that change in order to help them, not only will the lodge not do as advised, but they will get angry or see the one giving advice as the problem. In such a case, to continue to try and help will only cause more problems. You need to back away and allow them to see the problem for themselves or fail as a lodge.

We must do all we can to help anyone who asks for our help. We must also respect that everyone has the right to do as they desire. We should never try to force our will on another.

If we are in a situation that we know is not right for us and the lodge does not wish to change, then we should find a new lodge. If the lodge does not wish to change because they are successful in what they are doing, wish them well and move on. If they are in obvious trouble and you realize that if they do not change, they will possibly fail at some point, then take a few extra steps with them. Try to make them see that it is in their best interest to change.

However, we must realize that there is a point when offering help becomes harassment. No matter how much we may want to help, we must realize that sometimes the very best help we can give is to walk away. No matter how much it hurts, we cannot help someone who does not want to be helped.

By pushing our help, we may not only aggravate a bad situation, but we may be denying others who are ready and willing to accept our help. We must know when a desire to help becomes a desire to get our own way.

Walking away is sometimes the most Masonic thing that can be done.

Improper Use of Masonry

Not long ago I was going through some boxes I had in storage and found a box that I had not seen in many years. It contained personal items from around the time that I joined Masonry. One of the things that I found was a small booklet my lodge had printed just after I had joined. It was the lodge bylaws and roster of members.

Looking through the booklet, and the names of members long gone, it took me back to many of the events and conversations from that time. I remember one conversation with an elderly Mason who told me of how Masons sometimes interacted with each other during difficult times in our history — like during the time of the Great Depression of the late 1920's and 30's, or things that went on in the U.S. during WWII.

He told me of great shortages of things like sugar and coffee, and how so many things were rationed. Ration coupons were given out, and once you were out of coupons, well, you didn't get what you wanted. It was a difficult time. He told me that older Masons had told him that even things like white dress shirts that Masons would wear to lodge were rationed. He also told me how some Masons would bend the rules using Masonry.

They would sometimes wear their Masonic ring turned around so that the S&C would face their palm and go into a store or shop that they knew was run by a Mason. They would then ask for an item that required a coupon. When asked for the coupon, the Mason would not say a word, but instead of giving the coupon, he would turn his ring around to its proper position placing his hand down on the counter so that the shop owner could see the ring. Not a word was spoken, but the sale was made without the coupon. It was hard and difficult times.

I imagine that things like showing a Masonic ring may have been done out of a feeling that Masons should help each other. But when does it go too far?

I remember guidelines sent out by my Grand Lodge concerning linking Masonry to anyone's business. A Mason could be subject to Masonic discipline if he used the S&C on any business card or advertising for a business. It was felt that this was an improper use of Masonry and that the implied goal was to use Freemasonry for personal gain.

It was the same to link any Masonic symbol, lodge name or any aspect of Masonry to a business. Of course, I've seen some lodge rosters from the early to mid-1800's that not only gave the name and address of each member, but list his occupation, or place of employment. Is this only information on the member, subtle advertisement, or, maybe, a blend of the two? It's hard to tell.

Another area of interest is Masons in politics. Now, for as long as Masonry has existed, some Masons have served in political offices. Many Masonic history books clearly brag on the US Presidents who have been Masons, yet discussion of both religion and politics is forbidden in lodges at labor. So, if someone is running for a political office, where is the line not to cross between Masonic information and using Masonry for personal gain? I'm not sure that there is a clear line anymore — or maybe if there ever was a clear line. If someone said in a political speech, "Vote for me because I am a Freemason!" then I am sure most would agree that this has crossed the line.

But is it crossing the line to list Masonic Membership among the organizations to which a candidate belongs? I remember not very long ago a website came under severe criticism because it listed the names of Masons and their places of employment. It was a Masonic directory where Masons could list their names and places of employment for free. There were no lines of promotion for the businesses, only that this was where the Masons worked. A few Grand Lodges warned their members if they listed themselves on this site that they could face Masonic discipline.

Today I've seen some Grand Lodge websites that have exactly the same kind of Masonic directories. Different times, different attitudes? I guess.

When I first joined Masonry, one of my early mentors was an attorney by profession. He was well respected, but his business card was as basic as it could be. It was a white card with black ink and only contained his name, address, phone number, and the single line below his name: "Attorney at Law." He was aghast at some of the simple TV commercials from attorneys advertising their services. He told me that this was *highly* improper and did not know why the ethics board did not act on them.

He has long gone to his reward, but I sometimes wonder how he would react to some of the TV commercials from many of today's attorneys. Times do change and with it, some of the attitudes do change. So again, where is the line that Masons should not cross?

When are we providing simple, general information on ourselves and when are we using Masonic membership for improper personal gain? The answer is going to be subjective. When is someone telling a joke and when are they making fun of you? Usually, if something does not feel right, then it is not right. But, then again, everyone has their own moral compass.

The reason we have Masonic trial is because some Masons simply feel that they can do whatever they feel is proper, even if it goes against what most other Masons feel is acceptable. I don't believe that I can give a definitive answer. And, even if I could give a definitive answer for today, there is no guarantee that it would be valid tomorrow. Then again, even if my jurisdiction has a firm position, that does not mean it is the accepted position in other jurisdictions.

The best answer may exist within our Masonic teachings. There are times when we need to do the hard things. When we serve on an investigation committee, we are charged with admitting only those we deem to be morally worthy. But what does that mean? How do you know someone else's heart? Should we be kind-hearted and let everyone in? If we do that, then why do we need an investigation committee to begin with?

Freemasonry is not for everyone. To believe it is, is to misunderstand the nature and purpose of Freemasonry. Freemasonry is not designed to be an insurance agency where its members pay dues with the expected goal of reaping financial benefits at some point.

It is also not an association where its members use their membership to gain an unfair advantage over non-Masons in business or general society. We should be better than engaging in such activity. So, where is the line that we should not cross? How do we know when we or someone else has gone into that area that is improper for Masons to travel?

As with so many questions in Masonry, the answers are in our teachings. Pick up a book on Freemasonry. Read it. Then pick up and read another, then another. Don't stop. Ask experienced Masons in your jurisdiction. Call your Grand Secretary's office. Seek and keep seeking.

This is where you will find your answers. If your Freemasonry is only a club for fellowship, you simply will never find the answers you may (or may not) seek.

The Apprentice and the Master Piece

In the days of the old Operative Masons, becoming a Freemason was hard, difficult work. It was necessary for the Apprentice to show proficiency with his working tools, a willingness to work hard, and to possess an outstanding character. It was necessary for him to prove that he had the heart of a Freemason, be of lawful age (and that would be whatever age they determined), be sincere in his desire to learn, and be found worthy by use of an entire collection of demands required for membership. Also, he had to bind himself to serve under strict rules for up to seven years. The quality of his work during the time of his service was, in itself, a test of his character and ability. If he was found to be incompetent or unworthy, he was sent home.

From what we know of events during the Middle Ages, Apprentices in the Operative Guilds were taught the art of building as well as a study of the liberal arts and sciences. This was felt necessary to be a fully rounded Master Mason. Any perceived lack in ability, failure to properly follow instructions, or questions as to his character would end the young Apprentice's career.

During the early years, the Apprentice was given the most lowly of tasks and was in reality, little more than a servant to the Masters and Fellows of the Craft. If he proved himself competent and responsible, his wages could be increased. This would also allow his work and study to continue.

From what can be determined in the Old Charges, an Apprentice bound himself to live under many restrictions and have a sterling moral reputation and work ethic.

An apprenticeship might also end for offences such as being absent without permission, failure to be respectful to Masters or Fellows of the Craft, slander or even an evening at a tavern. Certainly, an Apprentice turning up drunk or with a hangover would end his association with the craft.

Their work was demanding and their life highly structured and restricted. The only hope of success was by diligent and proficient work, continually making personal advancements and following the many rules. After seven years of study & service, and *if* he was found worthy, he was invited to submit his "Master Piece." This was some piece of stone or metal that the Apprentice felt would represent his skill as a Freemason. It was his final exam.

The submitted work was carefully inspected by the Masters and if it was found acceptable, he was declared a Master. He could then be entitled to accept his tools and travel with the other Fellows on job assignments. But the Master Piece may not have been the end-all for the new Master. Continuing research on the old Operatives provides some interesting information.

Today, the degree structure of the craft lodge is Entered Apprentice, Fellowcraft, and Master Mason. But that structure may not accurately reflect the original design of the Operatives. In its earliest days, Speculative Freemasonry had only two degrees. The Master Mason degree was added later. But, while it seems that Speculative Freemasonry built upon the model of the old Operatives, there were some changes.

There is no evidence that I have seen to suggest that the old Operatives had a degree structure. They were basically working or not. It was a building trade. It was how they made their livings. Today, we view an Entered Apprentice as someone who is new to Masonry. This *does* match up with the Apprentices of the old Operatives. But how does the Fellowcraft and Master Mason degrees match with the system of the old Operatives. Well, they really don't. In fact, it seems that in the old Operative guilds, one was a Master1 before he was a *Fellow of the Craft*. This may be because these distinctions would have been in relation to their accomplishments and status within a guild.

Let's think of an Apprentice as someone who is in college. They are learning. At some point, they must take their final exam and if they pass, they will receive their diploma and be entitled to be called a graduate. This is the same as when the Apprentice would finish his studies and submit his Master Piece. If it was accepted, he would become a Master. He had graduated from his Apprenticeship. But a new college graduate does not receive a salary for just being a graduate. He needs to find a job in whatever field he has studied.

A Master in the old Operatives, had proven his skill and value, but he did not start drawing a salary until he was accepted into a guild as a Fellow of the Craft. In other words, he made money when he was hired. That's when he would start drawing his pay. A Master was one who had only proven his worth. He had graduated. A Fellow of the Craft was one who had been hired and began his livelihood.

So, with that understanding, the top dog was the one who was not only a Master but earning a living. Of course, in our Speculative Lodges, we have rituals for each of our craft degrees. The question must be asked. Were rituals of any sort used by the old operatives? The answer is a very definite; I'm not sure.

Certainly, rituals have been around since the dawn of man, and some have been associated with the Operatives. We have records of various ceremonies and initiations for pretty much anything that was felt important or significant. Submitting a Master Piece after many years of hard work would certainly seem to qualify as an important event. In addition, teaching by means of symbols is also a very old form of education.

That Speculative Freemasonry employs symbols in its education and ceremonies does not seem to be by chance. That we also have initiations is not by chance. I do believe that the old Operatives did teach many of their advanced lessons using symbols and did employ ceremonies, rituals, and initiations for their new Masters. I believe that the times when the Fellows of the Craft were not at labor on a cathedral or some other building project, they were using their time to advance themselves by means of education, ceremonies, and initiations. They were not just buildings stones but building the self.

There is another aspect of the Master Piece we need to consider. An Apprentice worked for many years to achieve his goal of being a Fellow of the Craft. It was hard, many times menial work, and he could have failed at any point. There were no guarantees of success. This was not, at all, a case of someone just showing up and because he was there, he was given positions or considerations. It was necessary that he prove his worth time and again. There was no guarantee that even if he were allowed to work all the way up to submitting his Master's Piece that it would be accepted. Certainly, many were not. There is a lesson here.

We value what we work hard to achieve. What comes to us easy is often of little value. The Master's Piece can represent the work or price that we must pay for anything in Masonry that we may receive. It's not about money; it is about the work we put into something. If we believe that fees or dues are the price expected to be paid, then we have missed one of the most important of Masonic lessons. If we believe that we are due anything simply because we show up, or that there is no need to learn the work because others did not, we are wrong. Anyone who believes such things has no real understanding of Freemasonry.

The work is necessary to sort the worthy from the unworthy. We don't build buildings. We build the self, and the way we prove our worth is by living what we teach.

Notes:

1. By the word *Master,* I am speaking of a level of achievement, not the one in charge of a lodge of Masons

The Role of the Masonic Writer
2017 Blue Friar Lecture

It is a pleasure to be speaking before you today — even electronically. Before I say anything else, I would like to apologize for not being able to be with you in person today. It seems that nasty weather caused my airline to cancel their flights to the area. But, through the magic of technology, I hope that this recorded video (finished not very long ago) will be a suitable substitute for my being with you in person.

At the start, I would like to express my sincere appreciation on being asked to deliver this lecture and be included among the Blue Friars. I am honored and privileged.

A few months ago, I was contacted by Brother Brent Morris and asked if I would deliver this talk. At that time, he asked if I might have a topic in mind, and we kicked around a few ideas. I was unsure of exactly what subject might seem most fitting, so we settled on my thinking about it for a while. During the time that I was giving the subject some thought, I received an email from a young Mason I've known a few years. He is one of the up-and-coming young Masons who is something of the more radical sort. He wants more from

Masonry than a spaghetti and meatball dinner followed by only a reading of the minutes. He wants — *the real deal*. He wants to learn the ritual, study the philosophy, and understand the history of Freemasonry. Radical, right?

I've known this brother a few years. I've read papers that he has written and enjoy conversations on our thoughts of Freemasonry. About a year or so ago, he asked me to speak at his lodge during his term as Worshipful Master. I was glad to do so.

Some months back this brother was asked to give a talk at a Masonic function. Unfortunately, I was not able to attend. But the reports that I received from those who did attend said that he did a great job. So, the mail he sent was not only surprising but gave me some cause for concern. He seemed to want to open up to me about the talk he gave. He said that prior to giving it he was very nervous, as he knew that there would be a number of Masons in attendance that he truly respected. He said that their opinion of his talk meant a great deal to him. He said that at the conclusion everyone applauded, but then he said that was it. He said that he was disappointed because nothing else followed his talk. He told me that he expected the brothers who he thought so highly of to approach him and speak with him about his talk. He said that he expected them to give him pointers or anything that he should improve. Basically, he expected them to critique his lecture.

I was surprised at this as it caught me a bit off guard. I stopped and did some thinking about various lectures, some that I've attended and some that I have given. I don't ever remember giving a lecture and having anyone come up to me with an unsolicited critique of my talk. And I've certainly never gone up to any lecturer and given unsolicited advice or pointers on how he should improve his next talk. This not only seems very inappropriate, but rather rude.

I was not sure what this young brother was thinking at first. I thought about dismissing the conversation. I then realized that this was a very sincere young man. I knew him to be a deep thinker and not someone given to emotional displays. I decided to think a little more about what he was saying.

Whenever I am trying to figure out a problem, I like to separate all aspects of the problem and put each aspect into its own little cubbyhole. I can then study the different aspects independently of each other and without interference. In looking at this problem, I thought about one aspect very quickly. This brother is creative. He is a writer. I'm not going to make a blanket statement suggesting that all writers or creative types are identical, but I will say that in my experience most creative people have insecurities deep within them. Even if they wear a mask or put on great displays of bravado, if you look hard, you can see that little glimmer of insecurity.

Most writers or creative types live with this insecurity as part of the creative process. This is what makes them continue and move to the next project. While they may seem very confident in everything that they do, and speaking now from personal experience, I know that late at night before sleep comes, little gremlins come into our minds and worry us. Did we do this right? Could we have done this better? Will anyone like this? Do I really like this? All these doubts creep into our minds and torment the creative sort. This is one aspect.

Another aspect is that unless anyone here has mutant powers like *Professor X*, we don't have the ability to read anyone else's mind. We know exactly what we think, but we have no clue what anyone next to us, or around us, is thinking. If we know someone well, or happen to be good at reading body language, then we might get general hints as to how they are feeling. If they are happy or sad — general things. But we can't get into another's mind and know exactly what they are thinking about something. That's the second aspect.

And then there is the third aspect. It is trying to understand how what we are doing is being received. Do they like what we're doing? Is it appreciated? This is a bit of a tricky one. Let me give you an example.

If I write a paper and that paper is published in some journal or other publication, that paper will go out to however many people receive that publication. Out of everyone who receives this publication, there will be a small percentage, and I have no idea what that percentage is, but they will take the publication, look at it, and then just place it down unread. If these people who do not read the article have any opinion of it, it can't be a valid opinion. How could I pay attention to any opinion anyone has of something I've written if they have never read it? So, this group must be discounted.

Then we look at those who have quick emotional reactions to anything written. This is also a small group. In my experience, they seem to be on both ends of the spectrum.

Some will be very quick to praise any and everything that's written. Others very quickly point out the "great flaws," criticizing much, if not all, of what is offered in the paper. In my opinion, quick emotional responses, either positive or negative, do not best serve us if we want an objective evaluation of our work.

So, what are we left with? We're left with a large silent majority who give no opinion at all about our work. So, if the majority of people do not comment on our work, and we do not have the ability to enter their minds to learn what they actually think of the work, and, in addition, we have insecurities and worry about the quality of our work, then I can begin to see this young brother's point. He is worried that he is either wasting his time because no one is interested in what he is doing, or that he lacks sufficient ability to properly do the work. His position and concerns are not at all unreasonable.

After some thought, I told the brother that always do my work by the "rule of one." What that means is that if I do something, I try to be as objective as possible. I look at my work and ask myself if I can truly see just one person benefiting or being helped in some way from what I've done. If the answer is yes, then I keep it. If I cannot objectively see anyone benefiting from something I've done, then I toss it away. I tried to explain to him that since we can't get into the minds of anyone else, we need to use our own mind to objectively evaluate what we have done.

But then I pointed out that there is another aspect that we need to consider, and it is the cold reality of history. Sometimes we might not ever obtain the answers that we seek. Let me explain. A few years back, I gave a talk in a lodge. There were about 35 or 40 Masons present. I wanted to do something different with this talk and wanted to gain some insight from them.

I told them that I was going to ask them a few questions and would appreciate their answers. I first asked them if anyone who has ever heard of Albert Pike would raise their hand. Like a shot, every hand in the room went up. I pointed out that Pike was a Sovereign Grand Commander of the Supreme Council, Southern Jurisdiction and most Masons in the US did know of him. I then asked them if anyone could tell me the name of the Grand Commander who followed Albert Pike. Nothing. Not a single hand went up. I was a little surprised as I was in a Louisiana lodge. I gave them a hint. I told them that he was the Grand Secretary of the Grand Lodge of Louisiana. Still nothing. I said, "Okay, does anyone know the Grand Commander of the Southern Jurisdiction right *before* Albert Pike?" Surprisingly, about a half a dozen hands slowly went up. I thought, "Okay, this is interesting."

I had some paper and pencils and sent them out to everyone who raised their hands. I asked them if they could write down the name of the Grand Commander just before Pike and then send it back to me. All the papers came back and to my surprise, each one of them had the same name written down — Albert Mackey. I thought, "How interesting." Albert Mackey was never the Grand Commander of the Southern Jurisdiction. But he did have something very much in common with Albert Pike. And I don't mean the Scottish Rite as the Grand Commander before and after Pike also had the Scottish Rite in common, but no one knew their names.

What Brothers Mackey and Pike had in common was that they were both prolific writers. They wrote and they wrote, and they wrote. They were also both human beings and had all the doubts, insecurities, and concerns of anyone today. Yet, well over 100 years after the death of both, their names are still known. They have an impact, even today. It was not the office which Albert Pike held that is the reason he is remembered today. It was his pen. It was his determination to write and keep doing it again and again and again.

Albert Pike had no more ability to see the future than anyone has today. He did not *know* that he would be remembered all these years after his death. He did it because he knew that it was the right thing for him to do. He wrote because he was a writer.

The pen is mightier than the sword. It's true. Those who are in positions of authority lead us. But it is the writers who teach the leaders. We, and I'm talking about everyone here watching this video, are the writers, editors, and communicators of today. We are the ones who will lay the foundation for the future of Freemasonry. It is an awesome responsibility. The young men who are reading what we write, what we teach, are the same ones who one day will be leading Freemasonry. If we do a poor job of it then we can expect poor leadership in the future. If we seek titles, glory, and honor, then we might just get it. But that will probably be all that we get. Time will forget us. History will forget us. If we are to do our jobs properly, then we must be unyielding, uncompromising in our integrity, and determination to not settle for anything but the best that we can offer. We owe this to the ones who read what we write.

I pointed out to this young brother that many well-respected and beloved artists, known today all over the world, lived their entire lives believing that their life was a waste and their work wholly unappreciated. I pointed out that our reward is our work. In the common understanding of fair and unfair, it may seem that we have drawn the short end of the stick. But truthfully, there is no work that I would rather be doing.

Through our work, we are living the teachings of Freemasonry. That's a reward so very few receive. My brothers, I encourage you to never stop what you are doing. It is too important to the whole of Freemasonry. We need to keep writing and teaching and never stop. I believe that what we do is needed now more than we might imagine.

Grand Abbot, this concludes my presentation. I am honored and privileged to be among the number of the Blue Friars. I'm grateful for the opportunity to address you. Thank you all.

A Dragon in My Garage

The late, noted astrophysicist and author, Dr. Carl Sagan, once told a wonderful story that I would like to pass on. He spoke of talking with a neighbor and telling him of a dragon that he kept in his garage. The neighbor was obviously surprised and even more so when Dr. Sagan invited him to his garage to have a look. Upon opening the garage door, the neighbor saw the various things stored in the garage but no dragon. Dr. Sagan explained that the reason the dragon could not be seen was because it was an invisible dragon. The neighbor suggested placing some flour on the floor of the garage so that he could at least see the dragon's footprints. Dr. Sagan told him that this would be of no use as the dragon floats in the air. The neighbor then said that he could bring an inferred sensor to detect the flames. "Good idea!" Dr. Sagan told him, but unfortunately the invisible fire is also heatless. Every time the neighbor presented some idea that could prove the existence of the dragon, Dr. Sagan countered it with some logical sounding reason such a test was not possible. Dr. Sagan then asks us what is the difference between a dragon that is impossible to detect by any physical or scientific means and no dragon at all? What is truth?

A difference between science and religion is that there is no expectation of actual proof in religion. The poet Khalil Gibran wrote, "Faith is a knowledge within the heart, beyond the reach of proof." In science, we seek to discover answers, but in religion we recognize that some answers cannot be found by scientific methods. The lack of ability to know something is, however, not limited to religion. I can tell you that I am right now wearing a blue shirt, but how can the truth be known? There are no cameras in the room where I am writing this and by the time you read it I will have changed shirts many times. How do you know if I am telling the truth? While a truth does exist, your ability to know it would seem to be impossible. I believe that within this impossibility of discovering all truth lies the foundation of religions. We recognize that some things are simply beyond knowing, accept that reality, and do not attempt to seek, or demand, proof with science.

Science does, however, give us clear answers to many complex questions. There is much that we can prove by science. It is here that balance in life is shown to be so important. Just because there are some things that have no satisfactory answers does not mean that we should not look for those answers in everything. If we were to accept *anything* claiming to be a religion with no test of fact at all, then we may fall victim to little more than a cult disguised as a religion. If we accepted no religion because every question could not be answered, then the hole left by the inability to answer all questions would remain empty. The peace given by religion is the balance we find between knowing and not knowing.

This all brings us to the point of this column. It seems that today we face a near daily bombardment of claims of "fake news." In truth, a large slice of the information we receive today is highly polarized, emotionally charged, and with little to no support. In too many cases, anyone can say anything and, with no effort made to establish or prove what is offered, it is believed or disbelieved simply by if we like or dislike the information. It seems that the old claim that a lie repeated often enough becomes accepted as the truth. Where is the balance or the actual "truth"? Do we believe that there is a dragon in the garage simply if we are told it is there?

Perhaps we should recognize that we cannot answer, by scientific means, many of the questions of legitimate religions. But in all other matters, be it in a Masonic history book, a political speech or news story on some social media outlet, we should expect to see verification of what we read or find it ourselves. Anyone telling us something without any effort to prove what is said or written should be received with great skepticism. If we believe, unproven, whatever is offered, no matter who says it, then in the end we are the ones who stand to lose – and possibly greatly.

Being the Worshipful Master

(Preview from *Seeking Light* by Michael R. Poll)

Thoughts often arise concerning the role and position of the Worshipful Master. How does a Worshipful Master maintain order in the lodge? How does he walk the line of maintaining authority but not stray into abuse? Experience is a very good instructor, but many times (too many for comfort) young Masons are pushed into this office with only a few years of membership under their belt. Good intentions and raw talent may not be enough if events happen to test them and their metal.

There are few things that can destroy a lodge faster than a Worshipful Master who has allowed power to go to his head or has allowed the position to control him. Many times, the problems come from a lack of understanding of the nature or responsibilities of the office and other times it can be personality quirks where one simply seeks and needs power. If there is a belief that your Worshipful Master is actually abusing his office, then you should first seek the counsel of Past Masters or District Officers to try and understand if actual abuse if taking place or if it is misunderstandings. One on one talks are often very helpful. If it is felt that the possibility of abuse is taking place, then it is a serious matter, and you should contact the District Deputy Grand Master of other Grand Lodge officers as they may be needed to see what steps can be taken to correct the situation.

There are certain things, in jurisdictions with which I am familiar, which are not allowed to be done by a Worshipful Master. One thing a Worshipful Master is not allowed to do is reprimand a brother in open lodge without a trial. If, following a Masonic trial, a Mason is found guilty of an offense, reprimand in open lodge is one of the verdicts that can be given. So, if a Worshipful Master did reprimand a member in open lodge and no trial had taken place, then this would be an abuse of his office.

A Worshipful Master should use care in his words and actions in open lodge. If, for example, a member of the lodge is speaking out of turn or in other ways disruptive, a tap of the gavel by the Worshipful Master and a reminder to come to order should be enough to resolve the situation. If this action is not enough to resolve the situation, then it is proper to gavel the brother up and remind him to come to order. If all else fails, the Worshipful Master can tell him, "Brother, you are instructed to retire from the lodge." While this action is appropriate as a last resort, it would not be appropriate to follow this up with anything like "You should be ashamed of yourself." "You are not acting like a Mason." "You must learn how to conduct yourself in lodge" or any words which give the appearance of a reprimand.

Abuse of power can create problems all the way across the board, and I have seen the destruction of a lodge due to the acts of an abusive Worshipful Master. If you witness such an event in your lodge, bring it up to someone. Let others in positions of authority know exactly what happened so that the matter might have a better chance of being resolved.

One of the clear problems that can lead to abuse of power comes from the speed at which a Mason can become a Worshipful Master. Realistically, someone can join a lodge and within just a year or two can be elected Worshipful Master. They simply have not had the time to learn all that needs to be learned, not only with the ritual, but the practices and laws of the jurisdiction. They have not seen enough problems in lodges and how the problems were resolved. But not only is there a risk of their being abusive, but it can also go to the other end of the spectrum, and they may not know how to be firm enough in the lodge.

Anyone who is in line for the office of Worshipful Master should try to attend as many lodges as are practical. They should expose themselves to as many lodge meetings as they can to maximize the number of potential problems and witness the resolution to the problems. They should read as many books as they can lay their hands on dealing with lodges practices, lodge procedures and, of course, they should be very familiar with their own Grand Lodge rules and regulations.

When you are sitting in the East, an odd feeling comes over you — especially when you are new to the office. It seems that everyone in the lodge is looking at you and watching every move you make. Every word you say feels under scrutiny. Nerves can come into play, and you may find it difficult to sometimes talk at all. Of course, you may find that the very best answers to questions or situations will come to you two or three days after the event has passed. It will only be then that you realize the best answer.

Regardless of nerves or insecurities, a wise Worshipful Master must realize that peace and harmony must always be maintained in a lodge. If a problem develops which can result in the loss of that peace and harmony, then the Master must take the steps to preserve the dignity of the lodge.

Let's look at an example of an event I personally experienced a number of years ago. I was visiting a lodge and the meeting was going along with no problems at all. The Worshipful Master spoke on how the air conditioning system had been malfunctioning and he called upon a committee that had been created to explore repairing or replacing it. It was an important discussion as either decision would cost a good deal of money. The chairman of the committee made his report and gave the recommendation of the committee. The Master then called for comments on the matter. Some spoke in favor of the recommendation and some against it. Finally, one brother requested to speak, and the Master gave him the floor. Instead of speaking on the matter of the air conditioning, he announced that there was an event with another body taking place the following month and he had tickets available for anyone who might want to attend. The Master, quite correctly, informed him that he was out of order, that the matter being discussed was the report of the committee and if he wished to offer his tickets he could do so after the vote of the lodge. From across the lodge a brother boomed out, "No! I want to hear about this event. Go on brother, continue letting us know about how to get these tickets." The Master quietly sat back in his chair and the one with the tickets finished with his pitch. I was dumbfounded.

After the lodge meeting, I learned that the one who yelled out his instructions was something of the lodge "kingpin." He was a Past Master who, for some reason, felt that regardless of who occupied the East, *he* was the true authority of the lodge. Everyone occupying the East understood his *position* and yielded to him whenever he required it. The situation was a failure from beginning to end. At the moment that the unruly brother boomed out his instructions, a responsible and experienced Worshipful Master should have dropped the gavel and instructed everyone that the non-related discussion was over as it was out of order. That would be the end of the matter in any reasonable situation. If a brother felt the need to continue to challenge the Master and would not allow the matter to drop, it would then be advisable, in his case, to place the lodge at refreshment and deal with the matter outside of a lodge at labor. A wise Master should do all in his power to keep disturbances out of a lodge at labor.

A successful Worshipful Master projects an aura of confidence that is backed up by his knowledge of the work and procedures. The Master is in control of the lodge, but he always seeks the balance between making it clear that *he* is the Worshipful Master and not being abusive. No Worshipful Master should be unfair, unyielding, or unwilling to listen to the consul of others.

Successful Worshipful Masters know the value of "taking a beat." This means that when something happens, they do not immediately respond. They take a beat, process what has happened and compose their thoughts. "What has just happened?" "What is going on?" "What is the best response?" If you take a beat when something happens, you have a better chance of avoiding a knee-jerk reaction and saying something that may have been better left unsaid.

In all cases, the Worshipful Master is responsible for the proper work of the lodge. Unruly members must be reduced to order. If no other solution is available, an unruly member should be removed from the lodge. In doing so, the Master should act in a firm manner, yet making it clear that his goal is to maintain order in the lodge and his actions are with the best interest of the lodge. It should never be personal. The Master should not be unfair to either an unruly member or the lodge. Allowing anything to go on in the lodge is not in the best interest of the lodge. Such weak leadership can result in the same failure of the lodge just as if the Master were an abusive dictator.

Of course, any step or action taken which goes against the wishes of what another wants can result in hard feelings. If bad feelings develop because one simply does not understand how Masons should act in lodge, or the proper role of the Worshipful Master, then the Master should take the extra step to try and talk with him. He should try and make it clear to the member that no attempt to single him out was being made; no attempt to hurt his feelings or be unfair to him. But the Master must realize that he is responsible for the lodge and keeping order in the lodge is necessary. When questions develop, then the Master should seek the advice of knowledgeable and seasoned Past Masters or Grand Lodge officers.

There are a number of books and resources available for Worshipful Masters to learn ways to avoid problems and make a successful year. Often overlooked aspects of demeanor, dress and tone of voice will play a part if the membership respects you initially or if you have an uphill battle to fight. If you do not know the ritual then there may be a presumption that you also do not know the rules and laws. When you make a ruling, doubt of your abilities may result in challenges. This is just another reason a Worshipful Master who is proficient in the ritual, who is professional in his dress and conduct and giving all signals that he is in control will have a far easier time than someone who is not really sure of what they are doing or, worse yet, does not care what they are doing. If you don't seem to care, they won't care.

About The Author

Michael R. Poll (1954 - present) is the owner of Cornerstone Book Publishers and former editor of the *Journal of The Masonic Society*. He is a Fellow and Past President of The Masonic Society, a Fellow of the Philalethes Society, a Fellow of the Maine Lodge of Research, Member of the Society of Blue Friars, and Full Member of the Texas Lodge of Research.

A New York Times Bestselling writer and publisher, he is a prolific writer, editor, and publisher of Masonic and esoteric books. He is also the host of the YouTube channel "New Orleans Scottish Rite College."

As time permits, he travels and speaks on the history of Freemasonry, with a particular focus on the early history of the Scottish Rite.

He was born in New Orleans, LA and lives a peaceful life with his wife and two sons.

Thank you for buying this Cornerstone book!

For over 25 years now, we've tried to provide the
Masonic community with quality books on
Masonic education, philosophy, and general interest.
Your support means everything to us and
keeps us afloat. Cornerstone is by no means a large
company. We are a small family owned operation
that depends on your support.

Please visit our website and have a look at the
many books we offer as well as the different
categories of books.

If your lodge, Grand Lodge, research lodge, book
club, or other body would like to have quality
Cornerstone books to sell or distribute, write us. We
can give you outstanding books, prices, and service.

Thanks again!

Cornerstone Book Publishers
1cornerstonebooks@gmail.com
http://cornerstonepublishers.com

More Masonic Books from Cornerstone

Living Freemasonry
A Better Path to Travel
by Michael R. Poll
6x9 Softcover 180 pages
ISBN 99781934935958

The Particular Nature of Freemasons
by Michael R. Poll
6x9 Softcover 156 pages
ISBN 9781613423462

10,000 Famous Freemasons
4 Vol. Softcover Edition
by William Denslow
Foreword by Harry S. Truman
Cornerstone Foreword by Michael R. Poll
8.5 x 11, Softcover 2 Volumes 1,515 pages
ISBN 1887560319

The Freemason's Monitor
by Thomas Smith Webb
6×9 Softcover 316 pages
ISBN: 1613422717

The Scottish Rite Papers
*A Study of the Troubled History of the Louisiana and
US Scottish Rite in the Early to Mid-1800s*
by Michael R. Poll
6x9 Softcover 240 pages
ISBN 9781613423448

Cornerstone Book Publishers
www.cornerstonepublishers.com

More Masonic Books from Cornerstone

In His Own (w)Rite
by Michael R. Poll
6×9 Softcover 176 pages
ISBN: 1613421575

Seeking Light
The Esoteric Heart of Freemasonry
by Michael R. Poll
6×9 Softcover 156 pages
ISBN: 1613422571

Measured Expectations
The Challenges of Today's Freemasonry
by Michael R. Poll
6×9 Softcover 180 pages
ISBN: 978-1613422946

A Lodge at Labor
Freemasons and Masonry Today
by Michael R. Poll
6x9 Softcover 180 pages
ISBN 1613421834

An Encyclopedia of Freemasonry
by Albert Mackey
Revised by William J. Hughan and Edward L. Hawkins
Foreword by Michael R. Poll
8.5 x 11, Softcover 2 Volumes 960 pages
ISBN 1613422520

Cornerstone Book Publishers
www.cornerstonepublishers.com

More Masonic Books from Cornerstone

Masonic Enlightenment
The Philosophy, History and Wisdom of Freemasonry
Edited by Michael R. Poll
6 x 9 Softcover 180 pages
ISBN 1887560750

**Outline of the Rise and Progress of
Freemasonry in Louisiana**
by James B. Scot
Introduction by Alain Bernheim
Afterword by Michael R. Poll
8x10 Softcover 180 pages
ISBN 1-934935-31-X

Our Stations and Places - Masonic Officer's Handbook
by Henry G. Meacham
Revised by Michael R. Poll
6 x 9 Softcover 164 pages
ISBN: 1887560637

Knights & Freemasons: The Birth of Modern Freemasonry
By Albert Pike & Albert Mackey
Edited by Michael R. Poll
Foreword by S. Brent Morris
6 x 9 Softcover 178 pages
ISBN 1887560661

Robert's Rules of Order: Masonic Edition
Revised by Michael R. Poll
6 x 9 Softcover 212 pages
ISBN 1887560076

Cornerstone Book Publishers
www.cornerstonepublishers.com

More Masonic Books from Cornerstone

The Freemasons Key
A Study of Masonic Symbolism
Edited by Michael R. Poll
6 x 9 Softcover 244 pages
ISBN: 1887560971

**The Ancient and Accepted Scottish Rite
in Thirty-Three Degrees**
by Robert B. Folger
Introduction by Michael R. Poll
ISBN: 1934935883

Documents Upon Sublime Freemasonry
by Joseph McCosh
Foreword by Michael R. Poll
6x9 Softcover 115 pages
ISBN: 978-1613423110

A.E. Waite: Words From a Masonic Mystic
Edited by Michael R. Poll
Foreword by Joseph Fort Newton
6 x 9 Softcover 168 pages
ISBN: 1887560734

**The Statutes and Regulations, Institutes, Laws and Grand
Constitutions: of the Ancient and Accepted Scottish Rite**
by Albert Pike
Introduction by Michael R. Poll
6x9 Softcover 194 pages
ISBN: 1613421168

Cornerstone Book Publishers
www.cornerstonepublishers.com

More Masonic Books from Cornerstone

The Story of the Ecossais Lodge of New Orleans
Edited by Gerry L. Prinsen
Introduction by Michael R. Poll
8.5x11 Softcover 198 pages
ISBN 9781613423172

The Bonseigneur Rituals
Edited by Gerry L. Prinsen
Foreword by Michael R. Poll
8x10 Softcover 2 volumes 574 pages
ISBN 1-934935-34-4

Chapter Rose Croix
by Albert Pike
Foreword by Albert Mackey
6x9 Softcover 108 pages
ISBN 1-453762-02-7

The Life Story Of Albert Pike
by Fred W. Allsopp
Introduction by Michael R. Poll
6x9 Softcover 156 pages
ISBN 1-453756-87-6

The Grand Orient of Louisiana
A Short History and Catechism of a
Lost French Rite Masonic Body
Introduction by Michael R. Poll
Softcover 52 pages
ISBN 1-934935-23-9

Cornerstone Book Publishers
www.cornerstonepublishers.com

www.ingramcontent.com/pod-product-compliance
Lightning Source LLC
Chambersburg PA
CBHW051737020426
42333CB00014B/1346

* 9 7 8 1 8 8 7 5 6 0 6 4 1 *